UNDERSTANDING
YOUR HORSE'S
WEIGHT

UNDERSTANDING
YOUR HORSE'S WEIGHT

Your guide to horse health care and management

BY SHANNON PRATT-PHILLIPS, PH.D.

*the*HORSE HEALTH CARE LIBRARY

ECLIPSE
PRESS

Lexington, Kentucky

Library of Congress Control Number: 2009936646

ISBN 978-1-58150-212-1

Printed in the United States
First Edition: 2009

Contents

Introduction 7

Chapter 1 *Determining Body Weight and Ideal Condition* 8

Chapter 2 *Energy* 22

Chapter 3 *General Feeding Guidelines* 34

Chapter 4 *The Importance of Weight Management* 54

Chapter 5 *Feeding to Gain Weight and Increase Body Condition* 68

Chapter 6 *Feeding to Lose Weight or Body Condition* 76

Chapter 7 *The Importance of Exercise* 84

Chapter 8 *Truths and Fallacies About Weight Management* 90

Frequently Asked Questions 96
Glossary 98
References 100
Index 104
Photo Credits 108
About the Author 109

Introduction

Weight management, in any species, is a touchy subject. Where their horses are concerned, owners tend to be very defensive regarding weight, condition, and overall diet. As it is the owners who provide the diet, they are often blamed for any weight situation that isn't "ideal." However, as with humans, defining the ideal weight for health — and feeding to obtain that ideal weight — isn't always easy. Nonetheless, weight management is extremely important for a horse's performance and overall well-being.

This book is designed to introduce horse owners to the concept of body weight and condition in horses. Because body weight and condition are results of energy intake, some background information regarding energy (calories) and general equine nutrition will be discussed. As it is important for horse owners to understand the concerns and health risks associated with body weights that are not "ideal," these issues are described in detail. Finally, some guidelines for feeding and management practices for optimizing body weight and condition will be covered.

Hopefully, horse owners will not take offense at being told their horse is "too fat" or "too skinny." The goal of this book is to increase owners' knowledge of general equine nutrition and weight issues and to understand that a fat horse is not a healthy horse nor, necessarily, is a skinny one. The ultimate hope is that all owners will learn how to take even better care of their horses.

Determining Body Weight and Ideal Condition

To determine your horse's nutrient requirements — particularly with respect to energy intake — you need to first calculate its body weight and body condition. Body weight is measured in kilograms or pounds. Body condition refers to how much or how little fat coverage an animal has, and it can be measured through both subjective visual inspection to obtain a "score," or through more objective and quantitative body measurements.

Determining Body Weight

The most accurate way to determine a horse's weight is by weighing the horse. Scales clearly give the most accurate reading and can detect minor changes in body weight (though it should be pointed out that weighing a horse daily will likely reveal fluctuations due to fecal loss rather than true weight). Although most horse owners do not have access to scales, they are fairly common at equine veterinary clinics and research facilities. Also, many feed companies own portable scales and can bring them to your facility to accurately assess your horse's weight and to find out how much of their product you need. If you run a relatively large boarding facility or have mares and foals whose weights you'd like to keep track of (because growth of foals should be monitored closely), a scale is a wise investment. An equine scale can be purchased for approximately $3,000.

Because of the need for some kind of weight estimate in horses (for determining the amount of feed, de-wormer medication, etc.), several research groups have identified equations to estimate body weight using body measurements such as heart girth and body length.

Body length is measured from the point of the shoulder to the point of the buttock. Heart girth is taken around the midsection, behind the elbow, and beyond the highest part of the withers.

$$\text{Weight (kg)} = \frac{\text{(heart girth) x (heart girth) x (body length)}}{11{,}990}$$

where heart girth and body length are measured in centimeters

or

$$\text{Weight (lbs)} = \frac{\text{(heart girth) x (heart girth) x (body length)}}{330}$$

where heart girth and body length are measured in inches.

It is also possible to get a reasonable estimate of body weight from heart girth alone, which has given rise to the popularity of "weigh tapes." Readily available for purchase at most tack and feed stores, these tapes are placed around the heart girth area. Incremental weights have been printed directly on the tape to give a rapid estimate.

The calculation of body weight (from both body length and heart girth) tends to be a little more accurate than using the heart girth alone (from a weigh tape), simply because differences in body length can greatly affect weight. For example, the weight of a horse with a long body would be underestimated if determined by heart girth alone.

Calculations specific for estimating the weight of growing horses are more complicated, and a scale is recommended to monitor growth rates in these horses. Weight determination in growing horses is more important for ensuring smooth, consistent growth patterns than for ideal "body weight" with respect to fat coverage. Rapidly growing foals can be prone to developmental problems and orthopedic diseases such as epiphysitis or osteochondritis dissecans.

Measuring "Condition"

While important in determining your horse's overall nutrient requirements, knowing how much your horse weighs still doesn't tell you if it is too fat, too thin, or in good overall condition with respect to fat coverage. There are a few ways to estimate condition or overall adiposity (amount of fat cover) in horses. One way is through physical examination of the horse and assigning it a subjective score of adiposity. Other more quantitative means include those derived from direct measurement of the animal.

Henneke Scoring

Since the 1980s, veterinarians and horse owners alike have been using the Henneke Body Condition Scoring (BCS) system to estimate fat coverage of horses. This system uses a scale of 1 through 9,

Regions where fat coverage is examined in the Henneke system

where 1 represents an extremely emaciated horse and 9 represents a grossly obese one. Areas of the body that are examined include the shoulder and elbow region, the ribs, the withers, the loin and tailhead region, and the crest of the neck.

Occasionally some people will use a 0–5 or 1–5 scale instead of the 1–9 Henneke scale. These scales would follow the sample principles in which the higher number refers to a fatter animal. The 1–5 scale is commonly used to evaluate dogs and cats as well as dairy cattle and swine.

Using the Henneke scale, a horse in good general condition whose ribs cannot be seen but can be easily felt is assessed as a 5. Table 1 shows the correlation between the condition score numbers and the expected condition of the various assessed areas. The scale is useful because it is easy to learn, but there are several drawbacks. For instance, it is very subjective; one horse owner might label a horse a 3 while another might label it a 2 or 2.5. This discrepancy generally isn't an issue unless different people are keeping records. For example, if it wasn't known that different people were scoring the horses, one might assume a horse has suddenly lost or gained weight. It is also difficult to use the scale when tracking a horse over time to observe small changes in body condition score. In this case,

Body Condition Scores

Score:	General Description	Neck Area	Withers	Shoulder	Elbow	Ribs	Loin and Tail-head
1	Poor	No fatty tissue felt; bone structure obvious.	Very prominent	Scapula prominent	No fleshy tissue	Ribs obvious	Spine and hip bones prominent
2	Very thin	Prominent bone structure	Prominent	Prominent	Minimal fleshy tissue	Ribs clearly visible	Spine and hip bones visible
3	Thin	Lean	Lean	Obvious	Minimal fleshy tissue	Outline of ribs visible	Moderate visibility of hip bones
4	Moderately thin	Some fleshy cover	Some cover	Moderate blend into body	Some fleshy tissue	Faint outline of ribs	Faint outline of hip bones
5	Moderate	Moderate fleshy cover	Moderate tissue cover	Blends into body	Moderate tissue	Not visible but easily felt	Back level, tailhead fleshy
6	Moderately fleshy	Fleshy cover	Fleshy cover	Well blended into body	Extra fleshy tissue	Spongy cover over ribs	Soft tailhead
7	Fleshy	Fat deposited along neck	Fat deposited along withers	Not obvious	Obvious fleshy tissue	Ribs felt with pressure	Soft tailhead; ridge beginning to appear
8	Fat	Obvious fat on neck	Not obvious due to fat coverage	Faint scapula	Fat	Barely felt with pressure	Crease down back
9	Extremely fat	Obvious fat and potentially cresty neck	Bulging fat; withers indiscernible	Bulging fat; scapula not visible	Bulging fat	Difficult to feel ribs due to excessive fat cover	Crease down back due to bulging fat on either side of spine

careful record keeping and photos can be helpful to monitor body condition score changes with dietary management.

Another problem with the Henneke system is that not all horses follow the chart smoothly. For example, some horses may carry more weight around their ribs but won't have much coverage along the hind end. Therefore, it is possible for a horse to be a 6 at the ribs but only a 4.5 or 5 in another region. In these kinds of situations, owners and clinicians must average the entire body's scores to obtain the horse's true overall score.

BODY CONDITION SCORE OF 1

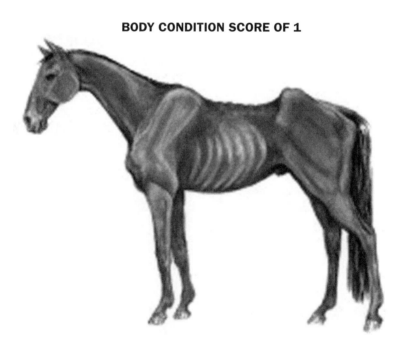

Emaciated

BODY CONDITION SCORE OF 3

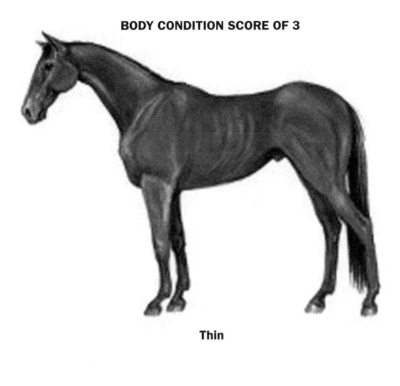

Thin

BODY CONDITION SCORE OF 5

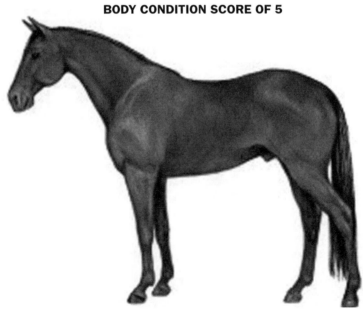

Moderate

BODY CONDITION SCORE OF 7

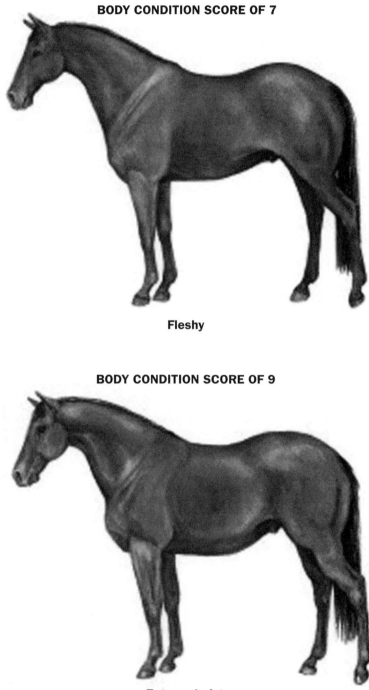

Fleshy

BODY CONDITION SCORE OF 9

Extremely fat

Cresty Neck Scores

Researchers in Virginia have established a similar subjective scoring system for the neck region, as horses with a so-called "cresty neck" appear to be more prone to metabolic dysfunctions such as insulin resistance. The cresty neck scores (CNS) range from 0 to 5, where 0 indicates no visible appearance of a crest (no fleshy region along the mane) and 5 signifies a crest so large it droops to one side. Most horses will have some tissue coverage along the crest (in the 1–2 range), and horses with more fat coverage will be in the 3–4 range. A score of 3 or higher would be considered a "cresty neck" (Carter et al., 2009a). It is rare to see horses with a score of 5 and a drooping neck, though it is fairly common in miniature donkeys. Ideally, horses should have a cresty neck score of less than 3.

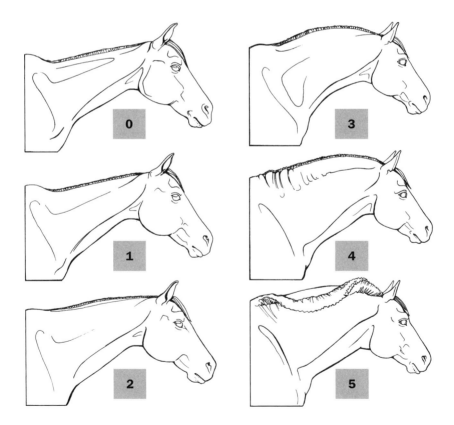

Quantitative Measures of Adiposity

Because estimates of fat coverage are subjective, researchers have been investigating more objective and quantitative measures of adiposity. For example, in humans the body mass index (BMI) is well-established to compare body weight with height to give an indication for overall fat mass.

$$\text{Human BMI} = \frac{\text{Weight (lbs)} \times 703}{\text{Height (inches)} \times \text{Height (inches)}}$$

A human BMI less than 18.5 is considered underweight, 18.5–24.9 is normal weight, 25–29.9 is overweight, and a score over 30 is considered obese. The waist-to-hip ratio (waist circumference divided by hip circumference) is another measure of body fat in humans and is particularly important as abdominal fat is believed to be more associated with health concerns than general subcutaneous fat (located just below the skin).

Similar ratios have been derived in horses. The girth-to-height ratio (G:H or girth divided by height) has been shown to be useful to estimate overall adiposity in horses and is well correlated to body condition scores. One study that examined these measurements (Carter et al., 2009a) found that horses and ponies had different ranges of girth-to-height ratios associated with obesity.

Another quantitative means of measuring fat coverage is with an ultrasound. A veterinarian or trained technician can measure "rump fat" on the horse's hind end using the ultrasound probe at a point 5 cm lateral from the midline of the animal at the midpoint of the pelvic bone (Kearns et al., 2002). The amount of rump fat is measured in centimeters. Then, the percentage of body fat in the animal can be calculated (Kane et al., 1987):

$$\% \text{ Body Fat} = 2.47 + [5.47 \text{ (Rump fat in centimeters)}]$$

For example, if the rump fat is 3 cm, then the total percentage of body fat is 18.88% (3 cm x 5.47 = 16.41, + 2.47 = 18.88). Most lean horses would have body fat percentages in the range of 8–14%, while horses with excess body fat would likely have values in the 16–30% range. It should be noted that this equation to determine body fat was only assessed in a couple of breeds of horses and may not be applicable to all body types. Nonetheless, rump fat (measured in cm) is still a useful measure of adiposity and can be monitored over time.

Ideal Weight?

So what is the ideal body score or level of adiposity in horses? At this point, veterinarians and nutritionists aren't certain. Most horse owners, veterinarians, and nutritionists agree that, in general, a leaner animal is healthier (within reason). In this sense, a horse with a body condition of 5 is generally considered to be in good condition. However, in some cases a leaner or fatter condition may be desired, as described below.

Determining an ideal weight for a horse is difficult, in part due to vast breed differences affecting bone and musculature. Muscle accounts for more than 50% of body weight in most athletic horses (and is usually still around 45% in non-athletic horses), compared to 30% to 40% in other species. As in humans, muscle weighs more than fat; therefore, a muscled horse will weigh more than a fat one for a given height and body type. Thus, it is difficult to make claims such as a 16-hand horse should weigh 500 kg. In reality, based on breed differences a 16-hand horse may weigh anywhere between 450 and 550 kg. This is another reason why body condition scores are useful.

Horses with body condition scores equal to or greater than 7 are considered overweight, while those with scores equal to or greater than 8 are considered obese. In terms of the girth-to-height ratios, a horse would be considered overweight if the G:H was 1.26 and obese if the G:H was greater than 1.29. A pony would be considered overweight if the G:H was 1.33 and obese if the G:H was 1.38 (Carter et al., 2009a).

In domestic species such as dogs and cats, it is well established that leaner animals live longer and healthier lives. One study in dogs found those that consumed 25% less food than their counterparts lived significantly longer (1.8 years) and had lower incidences of chronic disease (Kealy et al., 2002). It is unknown if horses fare the same way, though it isn't unreasonable to speculate that a horse with a body condition score of 4 may be very healthy. In fact, a leaner body condition score may be ideal for a horse with any kind of chronic lameness, as the amount of body weight on the limbs would be less.

In some cases it might be wise for a horse to have a slightly higher body condition score. The original work by Henneke studied reproductive efficiency in mares and found that mares with more condition (higher BCS) had higher conception rates than their leaner counterparts. So, it may be wise to keep a broodmare at a slightly higher condition (for example, around a BCS of 6), though keeping any horse at a body condition score greater than 7 may increase

One study found that mares benefit from a higher BCS.

the risk of metabolic issues (see Chapter 4). It may also be recommended that older horses be kept in higher condition (BCS 6). As the ability to maintain weight during disease or times of stress becomes increasingly difficult with increasing age, having a bit of a "buffer" in body weight could be beneficial. However, the overall health of the animal should be taken into consideration, as an older horse with arthritis or a history of laminitis may do better without the excess weight.

Only a few studies have reported body conditions of performing horses. It has been reported that horses competing in endurance events are more successful with more condition. Specifically, horses entered in the 100-mile Tevis Cup successfully completed 20 miles more with each additional body condition score; for example, a horse with a score of 4 averaged 20 miles more than a horse with a score of 3. Horses with body condition scores less than 3 did not finish the race (Garlinghouse and Burrill, 1999). From this it would be taken that endurance horses should be kept in moderate condition

Endurance horses should be kept at a moderate condition.

(BCS 4–5). Most racehorses are reported to be in the 3.5–5 range, though it is unknown how this relates to overall performance. Pagan and coworkers (2009) reported body condition scores in sporthorses and found that pony hunters had average scores of 7; dressage, hunters, and jumpers had average scores ranging from 5.5–6.5; and polo horses were close to 5.

Horse owners should work with their veterinarians and trainers to determine the ideal body condition for their horse and discipline, as serious consequences can result when a horse is too thin or too fat (see Chapter 4). However, prior to discussing health concerns regarding weight management, the concept of energy balance must be introduced.

CHAPTER 2

Energy

Understanding the concept of weight management requires an understanding of energy. Very often horse owners confuse the term "energy" with "spirit" or "activity level." As it relates to nutrition, however, energy refers to calories, which are units of energy (described further below). And with respect to weight management, if any animal takes in more calories than it expends, it will gain weight (mostly as fat); if it expends more calories than it takes in, it will lose weight.

So what is a calorie? A calorie is defined as the energy required to heat one gram of water one degree centigrade. One calorie is a very small amount of energy; for instance, a 500 kg horse trotting for one minute burns 56,000 calories. Because a calorie is such a small unit of energy, most feeds and requirements are reported in kilocalories (kcal, where 1 kcal = 1,000 calories) or even megacalories (Mcal, where 1 Mcal = 1,000 kcal). To put it in perspective, humans refer to Calories (note the capital "C"), which actually represent kilocalories. Most equine diets are built on the range of megacalories. For example, a mature horse might require 16 Mcal of energy per day. In Europe and elsewhere in the world, the unit of measure for energy is the joule (J), where 1 calorie is equal to 4.184 joules.

The use of calories in equine nutrition is twofold: We discuss how many calories are required in a given day and how many calories are in feed.

Energy Content of Feeds

Horses derive calories by breaking down feed through processes of digestion, absorption, and metabolism. Different feeds will generate different amounts of calories per unit weight based on these processes, so it is important to have an understanding of how feeds are broken down. Some biochemistry is involved to fully understand these processes, so we'll just cover the basics.

Horses can generate energy from three main classes of feedstuffs: carbohydrates (derivatives of sugar), fats, and proteins. These are types of organic compounds because their structures have three key elements: carbon, oxygen, and hydrogen. (Note "organic" in this case does not mean "not treated with pesticides or herbicides." In the realm of nutrition, organic refers to compounds containing these elements.) Structurally, carbohydrates, proteins, and fats are very different, but the ultimate energetic end product of their digestion and metabolism is the same: adenosine triphosphate (ATP), with a difference among these energetic compounds being the number of ATPs each generates.

ATP is the compound required for muscle to function, though in reality it relaxes the muscle after a contraction. Continuous work (such as walking or trotting or even beating the heart) requires multiple contraction and relaxation cycles and substantial amounts of ATP. Thus, without ATP the muscle would contract but not relax. For example, when rigor mortis sets in after death, it is due to the body's inability to reproduce ATP to relax the muscles. (Eventually, the muscle proteins begin to break down so that rigor mortis only lasts a few hours.)

ATP is the energy currency of all cells, similar to gas in a car. Without gas the car wouldn't go very far. Likewise, the body needs constant replenishment of ATP, which we can generate through the metabolism of feedstuffs. Carbohydrates (found in forages and grains) and fats (found in small amounts in all feeds, but primarily in oils) are the most important sources of energy for a horse because of the ability of carbohydrates and fats to generate ATP through their metabolism. The use of one unit of ATP generates 7 kcal (or Calories) of energy.

Carbohydrates are extremely important to the horse for two main reasons. For one, they are a major component of forages, a staple of the horse's diet and required for digestive health. Secondly, forages provide ample energy for the horse after its digestion and metabolism to ATP.

One of the simplest carbohydrates is a monosaccharide, a structure comprising six carbon atoms arranged with hydrogen and oxygen atoms. Types of monosaccharides include glucose, fructose, and galactose, depending on the actual structure. Another type of carbohydrate is a disaccharide, such as sucrose and lactose, which contains two monosaccharides. For example, sucrose is made of the monosaccharides fructose and glucose while lactose is made from galactose and fructose.

A polysaccharide is a long chain of hundreds to thousands of monosaccharides bound together. Polysaccharides such as starch and cellulose (a type of fiber) are digested by the body differently, largely because of the specific bonds between the individual saccharides. Digestion of carbohydrates such as starch and lactose is through the action of digestive enzymes, which break these compounds into monosaccharides which are then absorbed by the body. Therefore, monosaccharides, such as glucose, are the primary form of carbohydrates ultimately used for energy production. Because of their relatively simple structure, sugars don't generate large amounts of energy (ATP) per unit weight. However, as horses can consume significant amounts of carbohydrates, particularly when fed a high starch diet (for example, one that is high in cereal grains), energy derived from them can make up a substantial portion of their intake.

Note that fiber, a type of polysaccharide, is not digested by enzymes produced by mammals. These carbohydrates must be fermented by microbial organisms found in the digestive tracts of most herbivores. The end products of microbial fermentation of fiber are the volatile fatty acids (VFAs). These compounds are absorbed and metabolized within the body and can be used to produce ATP. The VFAs do not produce substantial energy per unit weight, but have the ability to provide a large portion of the horse's energy intake because of the high intake of fiber in the horse's typical diet. The concept of fiber digestion is explained in more detail within the digestion section below.

As indicated earlier, fats are another important source of energy to the horse because of their ability to produce large amounts of ATP. Fats (lipids) are a category of nutrients that generally consists of triglycerides. Triglycerides are structures consisting of three fatty acid chains and one glycerol (a short carbohydrate) unit. Different types of fat are derived from differences in the fatty acid chain. For example, saturated fats have single bonds between all of their carbon units while unsaturated fats have double bonds between many of their carbons. The chain location of these double bonds gives rise to the "omega" fatty acids; for example, omega-3 fatty acids have their first double bond after the third carbon. Because of the complex structure of fats, their metabolism generates relatively large amounts of energy (ATP) per unit weight.

Proteins can also be used for energy production, though they are not a very efficient source of energy. Protein is found in varying amounts in most equine feeds, with feeds such as soybean meal and legume hays having high amounts (soybean meal is 44% protein and legume hays are typically 15% to 18% protein). Proteins are unique organic compounds in that along with the elements oxygen, hydrogen, and carbon, they also have nitrogen in their structure. Proteins are actually long chains of individual amino acids bound together. Amino acids are the building blocks of protein, similar to letters in a word. There are approximately 20 different amino acids due to different side chains in their structure. Proteins (amino acids) are primarily used to build tissue protein, hormones, and other important functional compounds within the body, but they can be metabolized to generate energy if fed in excess. However, before the amino acids can be utilized for energy, the excess nitrogen must be excreted from the body in urine. This is why feeding a high protein diet results in a smelly stall; the excess nitrogen excreted in the urine is converted to ammonia. When protein is fed in the diet, it will first be used to satisfy body protein requirements (See Chapter 3); any excess protein is metabolized for energy. Therefore, while protein can be used for energy, it is not a very efficient source of ATPs.

Feeding straight glucose, protein, or any carbohydrate to a horse is rare. Almost all equine feeds are going to have a mixture of some carbohydrate, fat, and protein, and the proportions of these will partially determine how much energy can be generated. However, an important part of the picture is how well these compounds are digested and absorbed into the body. The concept of how well energy is digested is relatively simple in theory. All energetic compounds (carbohydrate, fat, protein) can generate energy; that is, they can generate calories or heat when they are combusted (burned). The amount of heat (energy) generated by combusting a particular feed component is termed the gross energy. The gross energy of 1 gram of carbohydrate (straight table sugar, starch, or cellulose) is approximately 4 Calories; 1 gram of fat generates approximately 9 Calories; and protein generates approximately 5 Calories. Remember, however, that most horse feeds (such as grains or hay) are going to be made of plant material that already has a mixture of some carbohydrate, protein, and fat in it, so the actual gross energy of a feedstuff may vary. As the animal digests feed, some components may not be digested well and will be lost from the body as feces. The amount of energy digested (and therefore available) by the horse after energy is lost through feces is termed the digestible energy. Thus, the amount of digestible energy in a particular feedstuff is going to depend primarily on the energetic nutrients in the feed (fat, carbohydrate, and protein breakdown) but also on the amount digested. When we refer to how much energy a horse needs in its diet, we use digestible energy values. It should be noted that some countries use the net energy system, which accounts for losses of energy in urine, gas, and heat. Additional information regarding energy flow is shown below.

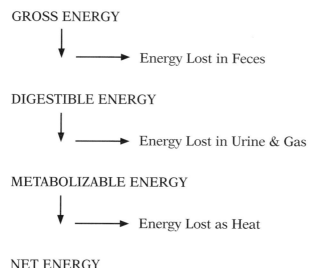

GROSS ENERGY

⟶ Energy Lost in Feces

DIGESTIBLE ENERGY

⟶ Energy Lost in Urine & Gas

METABOLIZABLE ENERGY

⟶ Energy Lost as Heat

NET ENERGY

The Equine Digestive System and Digestible Energy

The horse has a complicated digestive system. It has a relatively small stomach, about the size of the football. The small stomach lends itself to the horse being a "trickle feeder"; horses prefer small meals often. Food does not stay in the stomach long, but a rapidly eaten large meal does have the potential to cause gastric rupture. After leaving the stomach, food enters the small intestine (with segments of the small intestine being the duodenum, jejunum, and ileum). Here, a multitude of enzymes breaks most feedstuffs into small particles for absorption into the bloodstream. After leaving the small intestines, the particles that remain reach the large intestines. The horse has a unique section of the large intestine called the cecum. This is the equine anatomic equivalent of the human appendix, though functionally it is quite different. The cecum is approximately 3 to 4 feet in length and is important for fiber (cellulose) digestion. Also within the large intestine are the large and small colons. These are also important for fiber digestion as well as for water absorption.

From a digestive standpoint the small intestine easily digests simpler carbohydrates (starches and sugars) but cannot digest more complex ones such as fiber. As introduced earlier, mammals do not have the enzymes required to break the special bonds between fiber's monosaccharide units. Therefore, herbivores such as horses and cattle have formed symbiotic relationships with microbial organisms such as bacteria that possess these enzymes. This microbial population resides within the large intestine (cecum and large colon primarily) of the horse, while they reside in the rumen of cattle and other ruminant animals. These microbes actually ferment fiber into volatile fatty acids (VFAs). These volatile acids include primarily acetate (acetic acid), propionate (propionic acid), and butyrate (butyric acid), but lactate (lactic acid) may also be produced. After absorption, the metabolism of acetate and butyrate is similar to fatty acid chains, and propionate is metabolized to glucose in the liver. Ultimately all volatile fatty acids can be metabolized to ATP. It should be noted that during the fermentation process, in addition to VFA production, some energy during the fermentation process is given off as heat or gas and therefore lost to the animal. Therefore, carbohydrates such as starch and sugar are digested more efficiently in the small intestine and ultimately provide more digestible energy (per unit weight) for the horse than does fiber (because some energy is lost during fermentation prior to producing the VFAs).

It should be pointed out that horses have an upper limit to the amount of simple starches and sugars their small intestines can digest. So, if a horse has a large grain meal, there is a chance some starch and sugar would not be digested properly in the small intestine and would pass through to the large intestine. Here, the microbial organisms rapidly ferment the starch and sugar, produc-

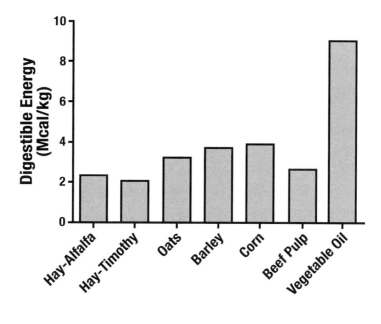

Digestible energy values of several common equine feeds. All feeds are based on 100% dry matter.** Both the alfalfa and timothy are midbloom.

**Dry matter is determined by how much water is in a feed. For example, pasture grass has water in it, so it is only approximately 25% dry matter, while hays are approximately 90% dry matter. When we compare feeds, it is common to list the nutrients on a dry matter basis (remove water) to account for differences in water content across feeds.

ing excessive amounts of gas and acids (namely lactic acid) that can ultimately cause digestive upset, or colic, for the horse.

Fats are well digested by the horse, so that the digestible energy of something such as vegetable oil is very similar to its gross energy, making it a very good energy feed. Protein is variably digested, depending on the feed source.

Digestible energy values of several feed types are shown in the figure above. As shown, feeds high in fiber, such as hay, have relatively low digestible energy values. This is because fiber (cellulose) is fermented in the large intestine rather than digested in the small intestine, and fecal (or gas and heat) energy losses are high. Cereal grains such as oats, barley, and corn that are high in carbohydrates such as starch and sugar are easily digested in the small intestine and have lower fecal energy losses. Therefore, grains have more digestible energy per unit weight than forages. Beet pulp is unique in that it actually has high levels of fiber but is highly digestible, generating a moderate value of digestible energy per unit weight. Oil is highly digestible and produces a lot of energy (ATP), giving it the highest value of digestible energy per unit weight.

Energy Requirements of Horses

To achieve optimal weight management of horses, it is important to determine how much energy (calories) they need per day. All animals need energy to keep their hearts beating, to maintain body temperature, etc. The amount of energy required to maintain normal body functions is considered the basal metabolic rate. This amount of energy is largely related to body size; thus, a pony requires substantially less energy than a Percheron.

The science behind energy requirements in horses is beyond the scope of this book, but *Nutrient Requirements of Horses*, published by the National Research Council (NRC) and the National Academy Press, discusses it in detail. The most recent edition (2007) gives energy requirements for three levels; high-maintenance, medium-maintenance, and low-maintenance. As most horse owners realize, some horses are considerably easier keepers

Ponies require less energy than draft horses, for example.

Horses in a cold environment might need additional energy sources.

than those that fail to maintain body weight despite large amounts of feed (the "hard keepers"). These hard keepers would therefore need the high-maintenance energy requirements and the easy keepers would need the low requirements.

The requirements discussed herein refer to "maintenance" energy requirements. An animal at maintenance is one that is not gaining or losing weight, is not growing, performing, lactating, or reproducing (pregnant mares, active stallions), and is in a thermo-neutral zone (the range in environmental temperatures where an animal doesn't have to change its metabolic rate just to maintain body temperature). For example, a horse in a cold environment would need more energy to maintain body temperature than a horse in a more temperate climate. Also, it should be noted that these "maintenance" values are purely estimates and that every horse is different. Nonetheless, these values provide a guideline for how much energy your horse needs for a given body weight. As will be discussed in chapters 5 and 6, feeding to have your horse gain or lose weight will require different energy intakes.

As indicated earlier, the digestible energy requirements of a horse

Energy requirements can vary depending on a horse's occupation.

largely depend on its body weight. The following equation is used to estimate daily digestible energy requirements of a horse:

DE (Mcal per day) = Body weight in kilograms x 0.0333

Thus, a 500 kg horse would require 16.65 Mcal/day to maintain body weight and a 400 kg horse would require 13.32 Mcal/day.

To estimate requirements for easy keepers (low requirements) and hard keepers (high requirements), multiply body weight by 0.0303 or 0.0363, respectively.

Therefore, a 500 kg easy keeper would require 15.2 Mcal/day and a hard keeper would require 18.2 Mcal/day.

Energy requirements for horses that are growing, pregnant, lactating, or working will be affected greatly due to the energetic demands of these processes. Such horses, including reproducing stallions, should be managed and fed differently and are beyond the scope of this book. If you need help formulating a diet for these types of horses, please consult an equine nutritionist or your veterinarian for guidance.

Now that we have our horse's estimated energy requirements, we can use this figure to generate a diet suitable to gain or lose weight as needed. The overall diet should still be considered, however, as well as general feed selection, discussed in Chapter 3.

CHAPTER 3

General Feeding Guidelines

With respect to weight management, balancing a horse's diet while meeting its digestible energy requirements is extremely important. However, a horse requires other nutrients that should be considered when looking at the overall feeding program. Any good feeding program will be based on the following principles: Meets the nutrient needs for the animal, maintains a healthy digestive system, offers feeds of the highest quality.

Nutrients Required by Horses

We have already discussed energy and how it can be derived from carbohydrates, fats, or even proteins. However, there are several other nutrients a horse requires such as water, protein, vitamins, and minerals. These will be discussed briefly, followed by information regarding equine feeds and sources of these nutrients. Specific amounts for each of these nutrients will depend largely on your horse's weight and activity level or physiologic status (such as if an animal is growing or lactating). Detailed values of these requirements are found in the National Research Council's *Nutrient Requirements of Horses*, and are summarized in Table 1.

Water

Water is by far the most important nutrient, and is most often overlooked. All horses should have access to fresh, clean water at all times. Without it, colic, dehydration, and even death could result. Horses' water requirements depend greatly on their physiologic state — as a lactating horse will require significantly more water than a horse at "maintenance." In general, a 500 kg horse will drink approximately 30–45 liters per day. However, how much horses actually drink will largely depend on diet; for example, a horse at pasture likely won't drink as much as a horse eating hay because the pastured horse takes in water with each blade of grass.

AT A GLANCE

◆ Mature horses need to consume *at least* 1% of their body weight in forage each day.

◆ All horses should have access to fresh, clean water at all times.

◆ Horses need some kind of salt source — either from a salt block or loose salt, a mineral supplement, or commercial feed that has salt added.

◆ Horses should be fed the best-quality feeds possible, suitable to their requirements.

◆ Consider calorie source — horses tend to do better when calories come from sources such as fat and fiber rather than from starch and sugar.

◆ Make any changes to the diet *slowly*.

◆ Get in the habit of weighing your feed so you know exactly how much you are giving your horse.

◆ Every horse is different — what works for one horse may not work for another.

Protein

Protein was discussed briefly as related to energy in Chapter 2 because energy can be derived from protein. However, protein's main function as a nutrient is to provide the building blocks for tissues, muscle, hormones, and enzymes. With respect to equine diets, we often classify protein requirements based on quantity and quality. Quantity refers to grams of protein required in the diet. Most horse owners think in terms of percentage of protein in a given feed, but how much the horse actually gets would depend on how much of that feed it gets. (Example: Feeding 5 kg of a 10% protein diet would give a horse 500 grams of protein [5,000 grams x 0.10]; feeding 2.5 kg of a 20% protein diet would also give a horse 500 grams of protein [2,500 grams x 0.20 = 500 grams].) Horse owners should consider the total grams of protein intake per day, not the percentage.

In addition to being aware of the quantity of protein a horse is getting, being aware of the quality of the protein is equally important. Protein quality refers to the amino acid make up of a feed. Some amino acids can actually be made by the body and are not essential from a dietary standpoint. Amino acids that cannot be produced by the body, such as lysine, are considered essential and must be provided for in the diet. A high-quality protein should provide these essential amino acids. Good-quality sources of protein include the seed meals (such as soybean meal or linseed/flaxseed meal) and legume (alfalfa, clover, etc.) hays. The essential amino acid lysine is of particular importance because of its requirements for growth. Some equine feeds are relatively low in one or more of the key amino acids, with lysine being considered the first limiting amino acid (an essential amino acid available only in limited amounts in a diet). Thus, if a horse were easily meeting its protein quantity requirements but wasn't getting enough lysine, the diet wouldn't be suitable. Let's use this analogy: If amino acids were letters, and protein a word (a chain of letters), lysine could be thought of as the letter "E"; it is very important for the formation of many words and certainly important in writing a sentence or paragraph.

Fats and Carbohydrates

The main nutritional property of fats and carbohydrates is their ability to generate energy through being metabolized. However, specific types of carbohydrates and fats serve additional important functions for the horse. For example, complex carbohydrates such as fiber are extremely important for digestive tract health; the microbial ecosystem is highly sensitive to an insufficiency of fiber. Furthermore, in humans it is now recognized that some types of fats are essential parts of the diet; namely the omega group fatty acids, omega-3 and omega-6. These fats are important for their anti-inflammatory properties and their roles in immune function. Horses also likely benefit from these omega group fatty acids and research is ongoing, though these fats are not considered essential nutrients (although they may be in the future).

Minerals

Equine diets require several minerals to meet a variety of functions including skeletal integrity and cellular communication. The macro minerals (those needed in relatively high amounts) include calcium, phosphorus, sodium, potassium, chloride, magnesium, and sulfur. Trace minerals (those needed in relatively small amounts) include cobalt, copper, zinc, selenium, iron, iodine, etc. Horse feeds tend to be variable in many minerals, and as they are usually low in sodium and chloride (salt), it is recommended all horses be offered some kind of salt source, such as a salt block.

Another important point about minerals is the significance of several ratios among these minerals, as the amount of one mineral in the diet may affect the use of another. For example, there should always be more calcium in the diet than phosphorus, ideally in the ratio of approximately 2:1. If this ratio is imbalanced, the horse may not be able to use the calcium in its diet and may develop bone problems. The only way to know how many minerals are present in your feeds (particularly hay and/or pasture) is to have them analyzed at a local agriculture lab. Most commercially available feeds will have minerals added in quantities to meet the needs of the type of horse the feed is designed for.

Vitamins

Vitamins are classified as water-soluble or fat-soluble. The fat-soluble vitamins (they can dissolve in fat) include A, D, E, and K while the water-soluble vitamins include the B complex (niacin, thiamin, etc.) and vitamin C. The horse is unique with respect to some of its vitamin requirements in that the microbes located within the large intestines have the ability to synthesize the B complex vitamins and vitamin K. The microbes do so in quantities sufficient to meet most horses' needs such that deficiencies of these vitamins are very rare and even difficult to induce experimentally. Horses, unlike humans (and fruit bats, primates, or guinea pigs), can synthesize their own vitamin C and therefore generally do not require it in their

Table 1: Nutrient Requirements of Horses at Maintenance

		Digestible Energy (Mcal per day)	Protein (grams per day)	Calcium (grams per day)	Phosphorus (grams per day)
Body Weight (kg):					
	Low	6.1	216	8	5.6
200	Average	6.7	252	8	5.6
	High	7.3	288	8	5.6
	Low	12.1	432	16	11.2
400	Average	13.3	504	16	11.2
	High	14.5	576	16	11.2
	Low	15.2	540	20	14
500	Average	16.7	630	20	14
	High	18.2	720	20	14
	Low	18.2	648	24	16.8
600	Average	20.0	756	24	16.8
	High	21.8	864	24	16.8

From the NRC's *Nutrient Requirements of Horses* (2007)

diet. Vitamin D, synthesized upon the skin's exposure to sunlight, is found in good amounts in sun-cured forages. Therefore, providing you feed good-quality hay (i.e., not last year's batch) and your horse gets some outdoor exposure, it should be getting plenty of vitamin D. Vitamins A and E are found in variable amounts in pasture and hay, with higher amounts found in pasture during the spring months and in hay that hasn't been stored for too long. Most of the fat-soluble vitamins will degrade over time in stored hay.

EQUINE FEEDS

Forages

Horses can meet their nutritional requirements through a variety of feeds, though forages are the primary source of most nutrients. Forages include hay and pasture and are the main part of the equine diet. Hay is the dried portion of the stalk of grasses or legumes and may be used to make haylage, hay cubes, or roughage chunks. Haylage is hay that has been placed in plastic (with no exposure to oxygen) and allowed to ferment. This feed can be very nutritious and is good for horses that are sensitive to dust. There is a small risk of spoilage and botulism, and horse owners may consider vaccinating against botulism if haylage is a mainstay of their horses' diets. Hay cubes and chunks are simply cubes or chunks of processed and cut hay, which may be easier for some horses to eat (especially if water is applied). Pasture and hay nutritive content depends largely on the types of plants it is derived from. For example, grass hay or

	Timothy	Alfalfa
Energy (Mcal/kg)	1.99	2.28
Protein (%)	9.7	18.7
Calcium (%)	0.48	1.37
Phosphorus (%)	0.23	0.24

pasture (timothy, orchard grass, Bermuda grass, bluegrass, fescue, etc.) has lower nutrient content than legume hay or pasture (alfalfa, clover, etc.), particularly with respect to protein and calcium. Season also plays a significant role in the nutritive content of the plant, with spring and summer plants tending to have higher nutrient concentrations.

While knowing the kinds of plants that make up your pasture and hay can give an indication to their nutritive quality, the best way to get accurate information is through a hay or pasture sample. The nutrient breakdown for representative grass (timothy) and legume (alfalfa) midbloom hay is shown on the previous page (in dry matter). As indicated, timothy is lower in energy, protein, and calcium than alfalfa. Either type of hay may be suitable for a horse, depending on its needs.

Taking a Hay Sample for Analysis

A hay sample is the best way to generate information about the nutritive content of your hay. It is very important to take a representative sample of the hay, which is easily accomplished with the use of a hay core sampler. The core sample allows the hay to be sampled

It's a good idea to test your hay.

from within the center of a bale (small rectangular or round) and allows all parts of the plant (stem and leaves) to be collected (if you were to simply grab a sample with your hands, the brittle leaves might be lost). Collecting approximately 20 small samples from many different bales will also give you a better representation of your entire supply. You then send your total sample (about 200 grams) to an agricultural laboratory for analysis. Your county extension office should have information on locations in your area. Most analyses cost about $20.

Energy Feeds

Energy feeds, those primarily fed because of their relatively high (greater than 2.5 Mcal/kg) calorie content, include cereal grains, beet pulp, rice bran, and oil. In addition to supplying calories, they also may provide other nutrients such as protein, vitamins, and minerals. Energy feeds (and commercially available feeds, described below) are often called concentrates because of their concentrated nutrient density (compared to forages). Cereal grains (oats, corn, barley, wheat) have variable protein and tend to be low in calcium. Furthermore, the protein quality (amino acid content) is not ideal for all horses. In most cases, cereal grains alone are not adequate for equine diets because of their nutrient imbalances, in particular calcium and phosphorus. By-product feeds such as rice bran or beet pulp are commonly included in equine diets to add calories. Vegetable oil is also another excellent calorie source, but it does not have protein, vitamins, or minerals, so it should be included in the diet carefully (so as not to "dilute" the diet). The nutrient breakdown of several energy feeds are provided below (dry matter basis):

	Corn	Oats	Barley	Wheat (Bran)
Cereal Grains:				
Energy (Mcal/kg)	3.84	3.2	3.68	3.30
Protein (%)	10.4	13.3	13.2	17.4
Calcium (%)	0.05	0.09	0.05	0.14
Phosphorus (%)	0.31	0.38	0.38	1.27

	Beet Pulp	Rice Bran	Oil
Other Energy Feeds			
Energy (Mcal/kg)	2.56	2.90	9
Protein (%)	9.8	14.4	0
Calcium (%)	0.68	0.10	0
Phosphorus (%)	0.10	1.73	0

*Take note of the calcium-to-phosphorus ratio of these feeds, especially wheat bran. Most commercial brands of rice bran have calcium added to optimize the ratio.

Commercially Available Feeds

Commercially available feeds are often a mix of cereal grains, by-products, protein, vitamins, and minerals. There are three main classes of feed form: textured, pellets, or extruded feeds. Textured feed or "sweet feed" has clearly visible individual grains and particles. Pellets are processed pellets of various sizes; and extruded feeds are processed even further with heat and pressure to end up looking like dog-food. These three forms often have the exact same nutrient profile (within a given class of feed), but are just processed differently. Some owners choose textured feeds because they prefer to see (and smell) the particles within the feed. However, some horses will sort their feed (spit out the boring vitamin/mineral pellet and eat only the grains) and would therefore be best suited for pelleted or extruded feeds. Most of these commercially available products are designed to be fed along with hay and may be chosen based on the quality of the hay (another reason why a hay analysis is helpful; it can help owners better choose the proper concentrate). Most commercially available feeds are relatively high in energy density, and have variable levels of protein, vitamins, and minerals suitable for the type of horse they are designed for. Some commercially available feeds are considered "balancers" in that they are fed in relatively small amounts (a few ounces per day) and are designed to balance out the nutrients (mainly protein, vitamins, and minerals) not present in sufficient quantities in hay alone. It should be noted that because balancers are fed in small amounts, they are not designed to provide substantial energy to the horse's diet (which is useful for a horse with low energy requirements). Vitamin and/or mineral supplements may also be fed if hay provides all of the energy and protein but maybe not the vitamins and minerals required. Also, a huge array of "nutraceuticals," herbs, or other supplements is available for purchase and may or may not be suitable for your horse.

Many companies design feeds specifically formulated for various classes of horses. For example, they may have a "mare and foal" diet, a "senior horse" diet, or an "athletic horse" diet. These products will have variable amounts of energy (usually 2.8–3.5 Mcal/kg), protein (8–16%), vitamins, and minerals specific to the horse's needs. It should be noted that digestible energy content does not need to be included in information provided on the feed tag, so you should contact your feed company representative to get this information.

Other Feeds

Protein supplements contain high-protein ingredients and are often included in commercially available feeds, or mixed with cereal grains to increase the protein quantity or quality of a horse's diet. Soybean meal, sunflower seeds, or flaxseeds are often fed for this purpose. The different seeds have different amino acid profiles, with soybean meal having the highest quality of protein, though animal protein sources (fishmeal and casein) have even higher protein and better quality. Flaxseeds (or flax oil) may also be fed because of their high omega-3 fatty acid content (note, the oil wouldn't have any protein). It is also becoming common for many horse feeds to have yeasts added to them. These are fed with the intention of enhancing the microbial population within the large intestines in effort to improve digestibility. While proven effects on digestion are minimal, they may be important for horses with impaired digestive function such as older horses.

FORMULATING EQUINE DIETS

The most important component of a horse's diet is forage, whether through hay, pasture, or a combination. The equine digestive tract is designed to deal with large amounts of forage; the microbial population is present to deal with the digestion of fiber; and the shape of the intestines (twists and turns) maximizes microbial fermentation, digestion, and absorption of nutrients. While the digestive tract is well suited to a life of grazing, it does not do well when horses are fed little hay or large concentrate (grain) meals. In fact, the risk of colic (digestive upset) is increased significantly with each additional pound of concentrate included in the diet. Therefore, it is extremely important that horse owners work toward maximizing the amount of forages in their horse's diet. If a horse doesn't consume enough true forage (for example if it has bad teeth and can't chew hay very well), other high-fiber feeds such as beet pulp or rice bran may be fed. A rule of thumb is that a horse should consume AT LEAST 1% of its body weight as (dry matter) forage daily. So, a 500 kg horse should consume at least 5 kg (about 12 lbs) of forage each day. Ideally, horses will be offered more than that (closer to 1.5–2.5% of their body weight, depending on the horse). Any concentrate offered (if required) should be fed at 0–1% of the body weight, and should never be fed in amounts exceeding the forage (except in growing horses whose digestive tracts aren't fully developed or suited for forages). Most horses will consume a total of 1.5–3% of their body weight per day, with the upper amounts being fed to lactating mares or horses in heavy work.

Most horse owners under-appreciate how nutritious forages are for their horses. The 5 kg of hay (even if it were the straight timothy hay described earlier) consumed daily by a 500 kg horse would provide 9.95 Mcal of energy, 485 grams of protein, 24 grams of calcium, and 11.5 grams of phosphorus. The requirements of this same horse (at maintenance) are only 16.65 Mcal of digestible energy, 630 grams of protein, 20 grams of calcium, and 14 grams of phosphorus. If the hay were offered at 2% of the horse's body weight, its energy, protein, calcium, and phosphorus intake would be in excess.

However, in many cases, hay alone will not provide the required minerals (especially salt and the micro-minerals) for a horse. Offering a trace-mineral salt block would be appropriate for a horse consuming only hay. If you are unsure of the protein content of your hay source, offering a balancer will help "top up" the protein in your horse's diet. A balancer (or at least a vitamin-mineral supplement) would also be recommended if your hay is a little older and its vitamin content reduced with age.

How does your hay meet your horse's requirements?

The graph below depicts how a horse's protein requirements are met with two different types of hay. For example, a 500 kg mature horse at maintenance easily meets his protein requirements when fed 7.5 kg (1.5% of body weight) of timothy hay. However, if this same horse were fed alfalfa hay, which is much higher in protein because it is a legume (compared to timothy which is a grass), it would be consuming far too much protein. If you recall, excess protein in the diet is metabolized for energy in an inefficient way and excess nitrogen is excreted in urine (this is why you might have an ammonia-smelling barn if you feed alfalfa). If we look at a yearling (weighing only about 320 kg, though it would be 500 kg at maturity), his protein requirements are higher than those of an adult horse. These protein requirements are not met with timothy hay, but are met with alfalfa. If you were to feed this horse timothy hay, a concentrate would have to be added to make up the protein in the diet, or simply more hay may need to be fed (it would depend on overall energy needs). This is the same situation for pregnant and working horses. In early lactation, a mare's protein requirements are so high

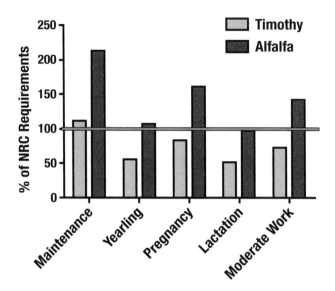

This graph shows a horse's protein requirements (500 kg mature weight) on different types of hay at different stages of life, when hay is consumed at 1.5% of body weight. The red line indicates 100% of requirements are met.

that even alfalfa hay doesn't have enough protein. This example shows that timothy hay is suitable for most horses, and that by feeding a little more of it, or by introducing some concentrate, protein requirements of most horses are easily met. Further, it shows that alfalfa provides too much protein for most horses.

Concentrate Selection

Concentrates (either cereal grains or commercially available feeds) are usually fed to horses when the horse does not meet its nutrient requirements through forage alone. For example, horses that are lactating or are in heavy work have such high nutrient requirements they physically cannot consume enough hay to meet their needs. Offering concentrates may also be helpful when training a horse (for example to come in from the pasture) or to mix in medicines or supplements. It should be noted that most horses do not need concentrates to meet their major nutritional requirements, as indicated by the previous example with the timothy hay. Most horses are in light to moderate work and can easily get their nutrient requirements through hay. In fact, the dependency on concentrates likely contributes to the high incidence of obesity we are seeing in our horses.

If your horse's needs call for a higher-energy (or other nutrient) diet, using commercially available products is a convenient way to provide one with confidence that your horse's diet is balanced.

Some horse owners prefer to mix their horse's feed, though it should be stressed that advice from a nutritionist be sought. Many horse owners, when designing their own diets, believe that if some is good (especially with respect to vitamins or minerals), more is better. Several minerals and vitamins are toxic to horses at relatively low levels, and it is easy to over-supplement. For example, an owner might feed a commercially available feed (which is formulated to contain the required vitamins and minerals), then feed a vitamin-mineral mix (again, with the some is good, more is better mentality). The owner might also then supplement with specific nutrients (such as a vitamin E-selenium mix). In this example, the horse may be getting three times his requirements of vitamin E and selenium. While vitamin E is relatively non-toxic (though it may affect the absorption of other nutrients), selenium is highly toxic at high levels. Working with a nutritionist is the best way to ensure your horse's diet is balanced.

Another aspect of selecting the proper concentrate concerns the source of the calories. In terms of energy, calories derived from fat are equal to calories derived from carbohydrates (of course, the amount of calories differs per unit weight, but a calorie is a calorie, regardless of source), though the feeds themselves can be quite different. For example, when a horse consumes a diet rich in starch and sugar (such as cereal grains), he will digest them into glucose. Some horses are very sensitive to glucose in the blood and will experience "sugar rushes" and will be "hot" after consuming meals such as cereal grains or high molasses feeds. This is very similar to a child's eating a candy bar and experiencing the sugar rush and associated hyperactivity following its consumption. Owners may actually want this kind of response in their horses, so it should be pointed out that the rush is very short lived (again, think of the crash after a sugar rush). Many people suggest their horses are becoming "hot," which really refers not to temperature but to temperament. For animals that are especially sensitive to sugar rushes and get "hot" easily, their owners should select feeds that do not contain very high amounts of starch and sugar. The feeding of fat or fiber does not result in significant glucose fluctuations in the blood.

Other problems with sugar and starch types of feed are their potential to cause digestive problems. As indicated above, horses have a limited ability to digest starches, so if high amounts of these types of feeds are fed, more and more will reach the large intestine. Here, the rapid fermentation produces gas, which could result in colic, or acids and toxins, which could result in laminitis. Remember, a healthy digestive tract often results in a healthy horse!

Starch and sugar types of diets also have the potential to negatively affect insulin sensitivity (discussed further in Chapter 4). The hormone insulin regulates blood glucose concentrations, moving glucose from the bloodstream into tissues such as muscle or adipose. If a horse frequently consumes sugar-rich meals, it will have many fluctuations of glucose throughout the day. With the increase in blood glucose comes an increase in blood insulin concentrations that attempt to regulate it. It is believed that frequent peaks in glucose and insulin contribute to insulin resistance. Because of problems associated with insulin resistance, it is becoming popular to see equine diets that are "fat and fiber" types of diets. These diets may have the same amount of energy (calories) per unit weight, but the body metabolizes them differently, and we don't see peaks in blood glucose and insulin. The feedstuffs in these products include things such as beet pulp, rice bran, and vegetable oil. Because horses may not fare well on grains and starches (in general, especially when fed at high rates), trying to have more of the calories within the diet coming from fiber and fat is probably a good option for most horses.

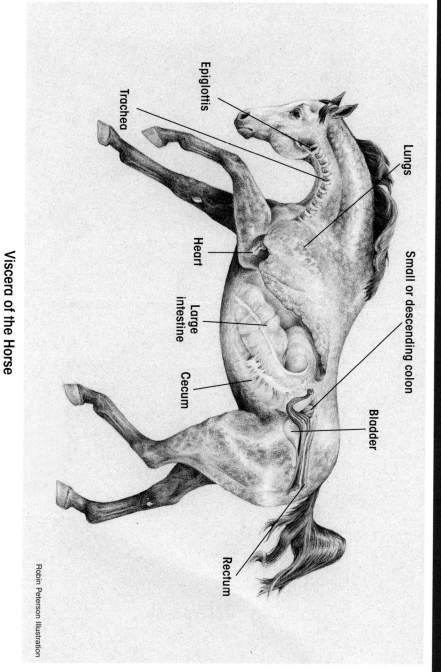

Viscera of the Horse

Epiglottis

Trachea

Lungs

Heart

Small or descending colon

Large intestine

Cecum

Bladder

Rectum

Robin Peterson Illustration

Obesity as seen in the donkey above and pony below
can lead to life-threatening conditions such as laminitis.

Among other places, fat tends to deposit in the neck, as seen in the horse above. The individual below checks for fat along this horse's crest.

The pertruding bones in the horse above indicate malnutrition.
Ribs are visible in the horse below.

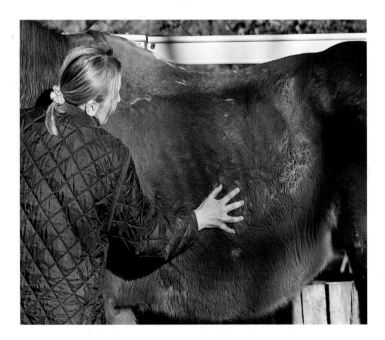

Meager pasture as shown above is usually sufficient for most horses and best for easy-keepers. In-foal mares such as those below benefit from good-quaity forage.

A tape measure can give you a good indication
of your horse's weight.
The horse below shows an ideal body condition.

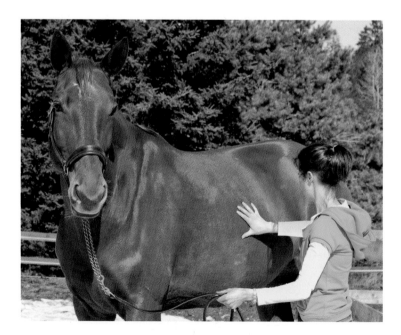

Knowing what your horse's diet contains and the right
amount to feed are important considerations.

A horse's diet depends on its use. High-performance athletes such as the horse above probably need more nutrition than the typical pleasure horse, right.

It should be pointed out that horses on a low-starch and -sugar diet *are not* on a "low carb" diet (a common misconception). Remember that *fiber* is a *carbohydrate*. And, if a horse didn't get fiber, it would develop severe digestive upsets and would not be very healthy. So fat and fiber type diets are not low carb, but they are low starch.

Feed Quality

Many horse owners confuse the concept of quality in relation to their horses' feed. Most horses do not need high nutritive content hay (such as alfalfa) and do quite well on lower "quality" hay. However, what hay (or grain or supplement) is fed should be of the highest value. Good-quality hay should be green and leafy and should smell good and be free of mold, dust, or other foreign objects (such as barbed wire or dead rodents). It is possible to have very high-protein hay (good nutritional quality) that is moldy and dusty and should really not be fed to horses, while at the same time you might have a low-protein grass hay (lower nutritional quality) that is fresh and green and palatable — and perfectly suited to most horses. Grains also should be of the highest grade possible, and more and more feed companies are looking to include human-grade products in their feeds. Horses should not be fed general livestock feed, especially feed designed for cattle, as compounds such as monensin are very toxic to horses.

Other Feeding Considerations

Any introduction of new hay or grain should be completed over at least a week, and ideally closer to 10 days. This gives the digestive tract and the microbial population a chance to adapt to the new feed. A good rule of thumb is that on days 1 to 3 of the new feed, the horse is fed 75% of the old feed and 25% of the new. On days 4 to 6, the horse is fed 50% of the old feed and 50% new; on days 7 to 10 it gets 25% old feed and 75% new. Then, by day 11 the horse should be entirely on the new feed. If you have a horse that has colicked before due to a sudden change in diet, this process could be spread out even more, with increments of 10 or 15%, instead of 25%.

As you may have noticed, most of the aforementioned feeding recommendations refer to weight of feeds (kilograms or pounds, where 1 kg = 2.2 lbs). To a nutritionist, weighing feed is critical for two main reasons. First, every "scoop" is different. If a horse owner says they feed "one scoop of oats," we don't know if this is one of the big metal scoops, a small coffee can, or some other sized object. Second, feeds have different densities, and therefore weigh different amounts. For example, 1 gallon (or other volumetric measuring device) of oats weighs significantly LESS than 1 gallon of corn. To add to this, the nutrients within each of those "gallons" are substantially different (because corn and oats have different nutrient profiles). Feed doesn't need to be weighed every day; once you know how much your scoop weighs, you can just feed by the scoop. Hay flakes can also be weighed to get an idea for how much hay is being offered. While each flake within a bale will differ, if you weigh a few flakes from a few different bales you can determine the average weight of one flake.

Calculating Dietary Intake

Doing any kind of simple ration balancing requires some math — or at least the use of software programs like Microsoft Excel. In an effort to determine what is in your horse's diet, you need to weigh all components of the diet, find out the nutrient composition of those feed components, and then compare them to your horse's requirements. Sound complicated? It isn't too bad!

For example, a 600 kg (where 1 kg = 2.2 lbs, so 1,320 lbs) horse

Weighing lets you know exactly how much you are feeding.

An example diet for a horse fed 8 kg of timothy hay and 2 kg of commercial feed

	Energy	Protein	Calcium	Phosphorus
8 kg timothy hay	15.92 Mcal	776 g	38.4 g	18.4 g
2 kg commercial feed	6.8 Mcal	240 g	12 g	8 g
TOTAL INTAKE	22.72 Mcal	1016 g	50.4 g	26.4 g
Requirements	19.98 Mcal	756 g	24 g	17 g

Note that the intakes of all nutrients listed are higher than their requirements.

at maintenance gets 8 kg of timothy hay and 2 kg of a commercial feed (with 3.4 Mcal/kg, 12% protein, 0.6% calcium, and 0.4% phosphorus). Simply list the nutrients of interest provided by the different feeds and add them up. Then compare to the horse's nutrient requirements.

Therefore, this horse is consuming more energy than his requirements and is likely gaining weight. While protein, calcium, and phosphorus are also above requirements (though the calcium and phosphorus are still in the desired ratio), they are not at a level of toxicity. This example demonstrates that this horse could easily consume only 1.2 kg of the commercial feed, which would bring the energy intake to 20 Mcal and would reduce the protein, calcium, and phosphorus overload. Alternatively, he could increase his hay consumption to 10 kg and very easily meet these nutritional requirements (10 kg of hay would provide 19.9 Mcal, 970 g of protein, 48 g of calcium, and 23 g of phosphorus), with no grain at all (think of the financial savings!). Obviously not all nutrients are accounted for but should be in a detailed dietary analysis. This example also shows how easy it is to overfeed our horses. It is no wonder more and more of our horses are becoming obese.

Calculating the above example is made difficult when a horse is kept at pasture. While pasture consumption rates have been estimated, it is likely that a horse will consume more pasture per hour if it is only turned out on a limited basis, compared to if it is out all day. For example, a horse at pasture for one hour per day may spend that entire hour eating frantically while a horse at pasture for 24 hours may just nibble throughout the day.

Understanding the Terminology

Nothing in equine nutrition is simple. When you take a look at your feed tag, it rarely indicates how many calories are in the feed. Instead it has all kinds of abbreviations. If you get your hay analyzed, you are left with a list of nutrients and "normal ranges" but with no understanding of what these are. The following are some key terms in equine nutrition (this does not include all of the information on any analysis or tag, just some of the key ones):

Acid detergent fiber (ADF) — A measure of fiber consisting mainly of cellulose and lignin. Cellulose is fermentable by microbes in the large intestine to generate some energy while lignin is entirely indigestible. Because of this, as the ADF value of a feed goes up, its digestible energy is reduced.

As fed basis — The nutrition breakdown of a feed based as is. In contrast to feeds expressed as a dry matter basis in which the water portion has been removed.

Ash — The total mineral content of the feed.

Crude fiber — A measure of fiber commonly used in grain analyses.

Crude fat — The amount of fat in the feed, also called ether extract (EE).

Crude protein (CP) — Estimated protein in the feed from the amount of nitrogen in the sample (nitrogen x 6.25 = crude protein). Includes non-protein nitrogen sources.

Dry matter basis — The nutrient breakdown of a feed with the water fraction removed. For example, if a feed such as hay has 10% water (the hay is 90% dry matter) and 15% protein on a dry matter basis, the amount of protein in each flake "as fed" is 14.4% (15 x .90).

Macrominerals (major minerals) — calcium (Ca), phosphorus (P), magnesium (Mg), sulfur (S), potassium (K), and sodium (Na).

Microminerals (minor or trace minerals) — For example: iron (Fe), zinc (Zn), copper (Cu), selenium (Se), and manganese (Mn). These are often expressed as parts per million (mg/kg).

Neutral detergent fiber (NDF) — A measure of fiber consisting of hemicellulose, cellulose, and lignin. Hemicellulose is well fermented by microbes (cellulose and lignin described above).

Simple carbohydrate fractions are another important part of equine nutrition, in part because of their ability to cause gastric upset. Some carbohydrate fractions are listed below:

Ethanol soluble carbohydrates (ESC) — Includes simple sugars.

Fructan — A type of carbohydrate indigestible in the small intestines but readily fermented in the large intestine. It is associated with laminitis when consumed in high amounts. Fructan concentrations are highly variable in pasture, with higher concentrations in the spring and fall and at the end of a sunny day (they are produced with photosynthesis). Horses sensitive to simple carbohydrates (for digestive or metabolic purposes) should avoid late afternoon pasture.

Non-fiber carbohydrates (NFC) — Includes starch, simple sugars, and fructans.

Non-structural carbohydrates (NSC) — The fraction of a feed that contains mostly simple sugars and fructans. It is recommended that horses sensitive to glucose in their diet (for mental, digestive, or metabolic reasons) be fed a low (less than 10%) NSC diet.

Starch — A polysaccharide well digested in the small intestine, though at higher intakes it may reach the large intestine where it is fermented rapidly and may cause colic or laminitis.

Water-soluble carbohydrates (WSC) — Includes NSC and starch.

The Importance of Weight Management

As introduced in Chapter 1, body condition, adiposity, and weight can affect a horse's overall health status. This chapter aims to identify some of the specific health concerns for horses that are too thin (emaciated) or too fat (obese).

CONCERNS WITH EMACIATION

The biggest concern with emaciation is overall undernutrition. In general, a truly emaciated or under-conditioned horse (BCS less than 3) isn't consuming enough nutrients. This could be because the horse isn't consuming enough feed altogether, or it is consuming feed that has a low nutritional profile. Therefore, in addition to consuming too few calories, the horse may also be deficient in protein, vitamins, and minerals, resulting in an unhealthy situation. While no studies of horses have examined the effects of limiting energy intake (while meeting other requirements) on long-term health, in other species it is well accepted that reduced energy intake resulting in a lean body type (approximate equivalent of a BCS of 4) is beneficial to overall health. With respect to horses, however, the general population interprets a lean animal as malnourished, and the incident can be highly scrutinized.

With emaciation — even if protein, vitamin, and mineral requirements are being met — the concern is the horse not having enough energy reserves in the form of caloric intake to function normally. Obviously, athletic performance will be hindered if there aren't enough energy reserves for work. In cases in which emaciation is coupled with increased stresses such as pregnancy or lactation, a low-energy status will be increasingly significant. The body will starve itself to feed the fetus, and in extreme situations the fetus/foal growth will be affected.

One potential cause of emaciation, other than simply insufficient feed intake, is related to intestinal function. Impaired intestinal function is most likely due to parasitic damage or colic surgery. However, there are cases of intestinal malabsorption syndrome in horses that result in idiopathic emaciation. (Intestinal malabsorption is a poorly understood condition where the digestive tract often isn't formed properly, and nutrients are not absorbed efficiently.) Colic surgery, which may result in resection and removal of parts of the intestine, can also greatly affect overall digestion. Depending on the segment of intestine affected, the horse should be fed accordingly. For example, if a large portion of the large intestine were removed, the horse shouldn't be expected to consume coarse hay; rather, the diet should consist of a higher proportion of easily digested simple carbohydrates and only highly digestible fiber sources.

If a horse has less condition than desired, it is wise to work with a nutritionist to determine if the horse's diet is providing the required nutrients. If the diet is adequate, then a veterinarian should be consulted to determine if there are more complicated reasons the horse is not getting sufficient nutrients. Tests such as an oral glucose tolerance test are often used to quantify glucose absorption from the digestive tract. Impaired absorption is highly indicative of malabsorption syndrome. In some cases of emaciation due to impaired

---

AT A GLANCE

◆ Lower body condition scores (less than 4) are often accompanied by reduced intake of nutrients other than energy.

◆ Moderate body condition scores (4-5) are ideal for horses provided that all nutrient requirements are met.

◆ Obesity results from taking too many calories in and not expending enough.

◆ The rates of obesity in our horse populations are on the rise.

◆ Obesity has several consequences including laminitis, insulin resistance, lipomas, and reduced heat tolerance.

intestinal function, it may be necessary to use intravenous nutrition (the direct infusion of certain nutrients into the bloodstream).

It is not uncommon for older horses to lose weight as they age. However, it should be noted that much of these changes are due to loss of muscle mass rather than fat coverage. While keeping an older horse in a suitable exercise program will help maintain the muscle mass, changes with age are inevitable. It is important for horse owners to realize that a lean older horse is not a bad thing, providing it is consuming a high-quality diet and it has sufficient energy reserves to face any challenges (such as changes in the season, work, or disease stress). However, as a horse ages, its teeth become worn and may not break down feed as effectively. Thus, horse owners should ensure that older horses get regular dental checkups and palatable feed. If not, the loss in weight may be due to an inability to properly chew and, therefore, breakdown feedstuffs.

This 27-year-old horse shows the faint appearance of ribs and a BCS of 4.5. Older horses often begin to lose a little weight, mostly due to reduced muscle mass.

CONCERNS WITH OBESITY

Obesity is a serious health condition, but, unfortunately, many horse owners still look at a fat pony and think how cute it is, or look at a fat horse and compliment its big bone. However, science has now shown that adipose tissue (body fat) is more than merely a storage organ for fat (and therefore calories). It is an active tissue that secretes hormones and inflammatory proteins that can greatly affect an animal's health.

Incidence of Obesity in Horses

Obesity in our equine population is on the rise, similar to that in human, dog, and cat populations. In fact, in the late 1990s the National Animal Health Monitoring System (NAHMS) of the U.S. Department of Agriculture estimated that only 5% of the horse population was obese. Recently, several studies have examined the current incidence of obesity in horses. A Scottish study found that 45% of 319 riding horses were considered "fat" or "very fat," with 10% of those horses in the "very fat" category (Wyse et al., 2008). A Virginia study examined 300 horses and found that 51% of them were overweight and 19% (of the 300 horses) considered obese (Thatcher et al., 2007). A similar North Carolina study examined 366 horses and found that 48% of the horses scored a 6 or higher on the Henneke scale and 20% scored a 7 or higher (Owens et al., 2008). It is no surprise that obesity-related health conditions are also on the rise.

An interesting secondary outcome of the Scottish study was that many horse owners did not believe their horses were obese. It is in fact common for horse owners to be very defensive about this topic. This further stresses the need for horse owners to learn how to score a horse's body condition properly and understand the health consequences of obesity.

There are many reasons for the rise of obesity in horses. One of the biggest causative factors is the lack of owner education about equine nutrition. Surveys have shown that horse owners generate most of their nutrition knowledge from feed dealers rather than from independent nutritionists, academics (professors and researchers of equine nutrition), or veterinarians. There may be some discrepancy in what a feed dealer suggests a horse needs compared to what a nutritionist suggests. For example, a feed dealer may suggest the purchase of a special feed for a horse, while a nutritionist might determine that ordinary grain will suffice, or even that hay is enough. Also, many feeds are marketed to improve health or performance. Horse owners may take such advice too seriously and overfeed the product.

Overfeeding of concentrates is likely at least partially to blame for more horses becoming obese. The importance of concentrates in overall nutritional health is largely overrated for most horses, but any equine trade fair is inundated with feed company spokesmen pitching products most horses do not require, and owners are often enticed by the latest, greatest product.

Another factor that may contribute to increasing obesity rates is that the quality (in terms of nutritional density) of feeds is greatly increasing, especially pasture. Today's pastures are mostly composed of plants intended for cattle and are too rich for horses.

Another factor contributing to obesity is owner perception of adiposity, and the fact that some disciplines, particularly halter classes, actually award horses that carry a bit of extra weight. Lastly, horse owners often overestimate the amount of exercise their horses get and underestimate how much exercise a horse actually needs. Horses can easily handle hours and hours of low-intensity work; therefore, a 20–40 minute pleasure ride barely scratches the surface.

Health Issues Associated with Obesity

But what makes obesity a problem? As indicated above, adipose (fat) tissue is no longer considered a mere calorie storage organ. In fact, adipose tissue is now regarded as a highly active metabolic organ that secretes hormones that play a major role in energy balance for the body and satiety (feeling full). Furthermore, adipose tissue produces inflammatory proteins called cytokines, which promote inflammation and can negatively affect the body. In fact, in humans, obesity is considered an inflammatory state due to the amount of inflammatory compounds produced by the adipose tissue. It is also believed that these cytokines play a role in causing oxidative stress, damaging tissues, and affecting metabolism, resulting in conditions such as heart disease and diabetes.

In horses, several health conditions have been associated with obesity, including laminitis. Laminitis is the inflammation of a network of blood vessels, known as the laminae, within the hoof — a very painful and often fatal condition. The inflammation reduces the laminae's ability to integrate and hold the hoof wall and the coffin bone together. Thus, with severe laminitis it is possible for the coffin bone to rotate downward and protrude through the sole of the foot. Laminitis can be caused by a multitude of factors, including mechanical trauma (like road founder or uneven weight distribution, such as what affected Kentucky Derby winner Barbaro), dietary causes (such as following the consumption of high amounts of grain or rich grass), and metabolic causes.

Metabolic causes of laminitis are those most likely associated with obesity, yet they are poorly understood. It is believed there is a complex interaction between cytokines and the vasculature (blood vessels within the hoof), resulting in inflamed laminae. In many cases, however, the laminitis is relatively minor and more of a chronic condition, termed founder. Also associated with this metabolic crisis is insulin resistance (discussed below). Insulin resistance, along with chronic founder, is often referred to as Equine Metabolic Syndrome.

Insulin Resistance

Insulin resistance occurs when the hormone insulin does not effectively regulate blood glucose. In normal individuals, insulin functions to move glucose from the bloodstream into tissues such as skeletal muscle and adipose tissue. Insulin does this by triggering the movement of specific insulin-sensitive glucose transporters (called GLUT4) from within the cell to the cell membrane. Once these transporters are at the cell membrane, glucose can move from the blood into the cell.

Following a meal, the rise in blood glucose concentrations (due to digestion of carbohydrates within the small intestine and subsequent absorption of glucose) triggers the pancreas to release insulin. As mentioned above, insulin functions to facilitate movement of glucose from the bloodstream into various cells, thereby lowering blood glucose concentrations back to baseline. When insulin does not function properly, an individual is said to be insulin insensitive or insulin resistant. In contrast, an individual with functioning insulin is said to be insulin sensitive. Insulin-resistant individuals cannot control their blood glucose concentrations. Therefore, after a meal blood glucose concentrations can be very high (hyperglycemia) and remain that way for several hours, causing the pancreas to secrete even more insulin in hopes of reducing blood glucose. The resulting high concentration of insulin in the blood (hyperinsulinemia) is a sign of insulin resistance. It is possible that eventually the pancreas can fatigue from its attempts to produce insulin and will reduce insulin production or potentially stop producing it altogether. This extreme situation is considered diabetes (when the pancreas cannot produce insulin, or does not produce enough) and appears to be relatively rare in horses. (Note: This scenario describes type II diabetes. In contrast, type I diabetes is a result of an autoimmune disorder in which the body's own immune system attacks the pancreas and its ability to produce insulin. This is extremely rare in horses, though a horse was born with type I diabetes in Kentucky in October 2008.)

Insulin resistance in horses is likely caused by a variety of factors. One potential cause is diet-related. As introduced earlier, diets high in starch and sugar are digested in the small intestine and absorbed as glucose. These increases in blood glucose stimulate insulin secretion. Depending on the composition of the diet, blood concentrations following a meal can vary greatly. For example, after a meal of "sweet feed" consisting of oats, corn, and molasses (high amounts of starch and sugar), there will be a much larger increase in blood glucose concentrations than after consuming a diet high in fiber or fat.

The increase in blood glucose following a meal is called the glycemic index (GI) and is a popular tool in human nutrition to quantify the glucose load of a meal. In equine nutrition the glycemic index of a feed is a little more difficult to quantify, in part because horses won't eat as quickly as humans (time of consumption can greatly affect the GI, and horses can't just be told to eat quickly). Nonetheless, in controlled studies, feeds such as cereal grains have been shown to have higher glycemic indices than feeds such as beet pulp, rice bran, or hay.

With respect to insulin resistance, it is believed that frequent peaks in blood glucose concentrations, and therefore insulin concentrations, dull the cellular receptors for insulin at the muscle or fat cell (think of living beside a train track: eventually with repeated stimulation you are dulled to the noise and don't notice it anymore). Science has proven that feeds higher in starch and sugar (and resulting in higher glycemic indices) lead to reduced insulin sensitivity compared to hay alone or feeds higher in fat and fiber (with lower glycemic indices) (Hoffman et al., 2003, Pratt et al., 2006).

Another important factor affecting insulin sensitivity is genetics. In human medicine, the quest for a "thrifty gene" is underway to prove that some genetic populations are more prone to obesity and metabolic conditions. It is well known in the horse world that some breeds are notoriously "easy keepers" and gain weight very easily. Furthermore, equids such as ponies and donkeys are known to have considerably slower metabolic rates, predisposing them to obesity. It has been scientifically proven that donkeys and ponies are less sensitive to insulin than horses. Breeds such as some warmbloods, Morgans, and Saddlebreds appear to also be less sensitive to insulin than are other breeds. One study found that ponies and warmbloods had higher resting insulin concentrations compared to some other breeds; however, it is possible these groups also had higher body condition scores (Owens et al., 2008). Researchers are working to examine this breed-associated factor to uncover a possible genetic link. It is also possible that gender affects insulin sensitivity. In a small group of horses, one study found that mares are less sensitive to insulin than geldings (Pratt et al., 2005). However, another study found no differences in blood insulin concentrations among 366 mares, geldings, and stallions (Owens et al., 2008).

Determining if your horse is insulin resistant is an important factor in managing obesity. However, regardless of whether your horse is insulin resistant or obese or both (a horse could be insulin resistant but in normal weight, or obese and insulin sensitive), it should be managed in a similar fashion; institute a low starch and sugar diet, reduce body weight (if required), and exercise more. If you have an obese horse with chronic founder concerns, he is likely insulin resistant, though horses that appear perfectly healthy have also been shown to have lower insulin sensitivity and may develop problems later on.

Diagnosing insulin resistance is difficult, largely because there is no clear indication as to what values of insulin sensitivity affect disease incidence. The most common method horse owners and veterinarians use to quantify insulin status is a single blood sample taken when the horse has neither eaten any form of grain nor has been exercised within six hours. Horses with resting insulin concentrations greater than 30 uU/ml are said to be hyperinsulinemic, though ideally the insulin concentrations are less than 20 uU/ml. However, research has found that these resting insulin concentrations are highly variable from day to day (Pratt et al., 2009). A single blood sample's insulin concentration would be a more credible diagnostic tool if hyperinsulinemia were detected in several samples from several different days. While hyperinsulinemia can indicate a problem with insulin dynamics, it does not specifically quantify insulin sensitivity (that is, it doesn't measure directly how well insulin actually works to send blood glucose into tissues).

Most of the tests that specifically quantify insulin sensitivity are rather complex and are used mainly by researchers studying the topic. The euglycemic-hyperinsulinemic clamp is considered the gold standard method of quantifying insulin sensitivity as it directly measures how much glucose leaves the blood in the presence of insulin. Other tests include glucose tolerance tests, where glucose is infused directly into the blood. Based on how quickly glucose is cleared from the blood, one can determine how effective insulin is. These tolerance tests are often used in combination with an infusion of insulin and mathematical modeling (called the "Minimal Model") to specifically quantify insulin sensitivity. These tests would be available through some veterinarians should a more definitive diagnosis be warranted.

The consequences of insulin resistance are profound. High glucose concentrations are believed to be toxic to tissues (glucotoxicity) and may directly damage the pancreas and blood vessels. What happens to the laminae with laminitis may be similar to situations in humans with uncontrolled diabetes, in which the development of gangrene in the feet is not uncommon. Extreme hyperinsulinemia has been shown to directly cause laminitis in ponies. In one Australian study, extremely high insulin concentrations (about 1,000 uU/ml) caused laminitis in all treated ponies (Asplin et al., 2007). It should be noted that concentrations this high are very rare (even most severely hyperinsulinemic ponies or horses are in the 200–400 uU/ml range). It is also possible that high blood glucose concentrations (even in the face of normal insulin) might trigger laminitis.

Overt diabetes, although rare in the horse, may be observed in extreme situations. The inability to use glucose (because it can't get into tissues due to either insulin resistance or diabetes) may contribute to impaired performance and a general unthriftiness. Signs of full diabetes include polydipsia (frequent drinking) and polyuria (frequent urination), as these are means to help rid the body of excess glucose (that isn't being used properly). Diagnosis of diabetes may include testing urine for the presence of glucose or testing for insulin in blood following the consumption of carbohydrates (insulin concentrations should increase with feeding in response to an increase in blood glucose, but if they remain very low or undetectable, diabetes is a possible cause).

Several studies have found associations between obesity and insulin resistance. There is a good correlation between body condition score and resting insulin concentrations, and it has been shown that horses with higher body condition scores (greater than 7) are less sensitive to insulin. The causative relationship between adiposity (the amount of fat coverage) and insulin function is not entirely understood. As mentioned above, adipocytes (fat cells) produce several hormones, including leptin and adiponectin, that likely mediate their effects on other tissues to affect metabolism. In horses leptin has been shown to correlate with both body condition score (higher leptin concentrations with higher body conditions) and resting insulin concentrations (higher leptin concentrations with higher insulin). Furthermore, concentrations of inflammatory cytokines have been shown to be associated with both body condition score and resting insulin concentration, such that horses with higher body condition scores also have higher resting insulin concentrations (suggesting some degree of insulin resistance) and cytokine concentrations (suggesting some inflammatory processes are at work) (Vick et al., 2007). In fact, measures of adiposity, as well as insulin and leptin concentrations, have been used to predict laminitis in a small group of horses (Carter et al., 2009b). At this point it is unknown if obesity per se causes insulin resistance or if insulin resistance contributes to the development of obesity. Nonetheless, the increased risk of laminitis associated with either obesity and/or insulin resistance makes this a very significant area of research. Recent studies in humans have further suggested that different regions of adipose tissue are of greater concern than others. For example, visceral fat, the fat surrounding the digestive organs in the midsection, has been correlated with insulin resistance to a greater extent than subcutaneous fat (fat just below the skin) (Phillips and Prins, 2008). It has been suggested that regional adiposity in the horse, such as the cresty neck or the

Note the obvious abdominal fat.

dimpling of fat in the abdomen or hindquarters, may further the risk of insulin resistance and laminitis in horses (Treiber et al., 2006).

Other Concerns with Obesity

In addition to increasing the risk of laminitis, obesity can affect other systems. Obesity in mares has been shown to cause disturbances to the estrous cycle, while reducing body fat through caloric restriction has alleviated these disturbances (Vick et al., 2006). It is believed that these reproductive changes are consequential to changes in the status of hormones such as insulin and leptin, though the mechanisms are not clear. This is in contrast to the original work by Henneke et al. (1984), which found that mares with higher body condition scores or those fed to gain weight had higher reproductive efficiency, and the work of Gentry et al. (2002), who found that fatter mares (BCS 7.5–8.5) continue to cycle through the winter months (which normally are anestrous for horses). Clearly more research is required to fully understand the interaction between adiposity and reproductive function.

Another obesity concern are lipomas — fatty tumors more commonly found in obese and older horses. They form along the mesentery of the intestines (the tissue that suspends the digestive tract in place). The tumors often are attached to the mesentery by connective tissue, which may wrap around the intestines themselves. Thus, either through direct blockage or strangulation, lipomas can result in colic.

Obesity also negatively affects horses' heat tolerance. Horses lose a great deal of their body heat through sweating. For an animal to sweat effectively there needs to be sufficient surface area (skin) for a given body mass. With obesity, there is a greater body mass without an associated increase in surface area (there will be some, but not to the same extent as the increase in body mass). Therefore, the horse must now dissipate more heat (due to a greater body mass) over less surface area. Furthermore, adipose tissue acts to insulate the skin,

More research is needed to understand the interaction between adiposity and reproductive function.

which is counter-productive for heat loss. This is a particular concern for horses working in hot environments, but even a horse that isn't in work may have problems dissipating heat.

Feeding to Gain Weight and Increase Body Condition

There are a number of circumstances in which owners may want their horses to increase body condition. It may simply be because a horse has lost some weight over the winter months from less access to pasture, or because it is a very hard keeper. However, it may be because of something more serious, such as recovering from illness, parasitic infestation, or from surgery. Then, too, a horse might be purchased or rescued without the

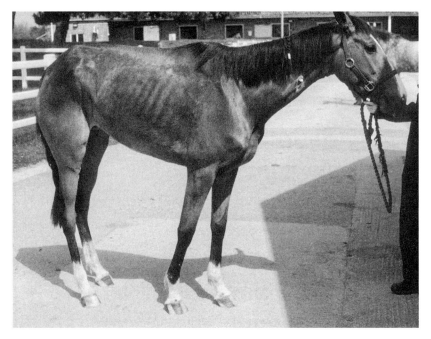

Illness or neglect can cause a horse to lose body condition.

desired amount of fat coverage around the ribs and body, or it may even be undernourished.

As mentioned in Chapter 1, horses should be in the body condition score range of 4–6, depending on various circumstances. Therefore, if a horse's body score falls below these figures, feeding to increase fat storage and

AT A GLANCE

◆ Increase the amount being fed slowly. Weight isn't gained overnight.

◆ Start by increasing forage and fiber sources before increasing concentrates.

◆ Fats such as vegetable oils are a calorie-dense and safe way to help gain weight.

weight gain is warranted. Occasionally, an owner may have a mare that is having problems getting pregnant and may require some extra condition (though ideally still no higher than a 7).

Horses in the 1–2 body condition score range are in a dangerous situation, largely because the associated lack of energy in such a condition has resulted from a lower overall nutritional intake, such as the lack of protein and vitamins. In these cases, nutritional intervention with the help of an equine nutritionist or veterinarian is strongly recommended. If you are unsure of the horse's history, it is wise to start slowly, offering increasing amounts of feed over several days. Remember that forage is the most important component of an equine diet; therefore, good-quality, nutritious forage (higher-energy and -protein hay such as alfalfa) is ideal. Concentrates should be introduced slowly to allow the digestive tract (and more importantly the microbes in the large intestine) time to adapt. In some cases, these horses are in such poor shape they have problems eating and even standing. Intravenous fluids and nutrition may be recommended in this situation.

Thankfully, most "skinny" horses we encounter are just those that could stand more calories included in their diet. It can't be stressed enough that any changes to a horse's diet should be made slowly, and this includes introducing more calories.

Energetics of Weight Gain

There is very little data regarding how much energy (or how many

Gaining weight can take a long time.

calories) a horse needs to gain weight. Furthermore, it is unknown if the same amount of calories a horse needs to move from a body condition score of 3 to a 4 are needed to move a horse from a 5 to a 6. That said, it has been estimated that one body condition score is associated with approximately 20 kg of body weight. It has also been estimated that it takes approximately 20 Mcal of digestible energy to gain 1 kg of body weight. Therefore, if a horse is expected to increase one body condition score, he needs to consume 400 Mcals more than he has been. If you think the average 500 kg horse needs only 16.7 Mcal/day (recall the equation to determine digestible energy requirements from Chapter 2), you realize that 400 Mcals won't get into a horse all at once. Gaining (or losing) weight takes a long time, and owners will have to be patient before results can be observed.

One way to determine how much to feed a horse is to take its current nutrient requirements (based on current body weight) or current feeding protocol and simply feed more calories. For example, if the increase by one body condition score described above were desired in 100 days, the horse could consume 4 Mcal (400 Mcal/100 days) more per day than it has been. If a more rapid weight gain is desired, feed should be increased accordingly. However, very rapid weight gain is likely not ideal, so be patient.

If a specific timeline isn't required, another simple way to have a horse gain weight is to determine its current nutrient requirements and increase its energy intake. For example, for a 450 kg horse the energy requirements would be 14.985 Mcal/day. To gain weight, the horse could be fed anywhere from 140% to 160% of his current energy requirements, or between 20.979 to 23.976 Mcal/day (which is more than would be required for a 500 kg horse). A horse that is naturally a "hard keeper" may need to be at the upper end of this range in order to gain weight. Alternatively, a horse could be fed to its desired weight, such that the 450 kg horse would be fed the requirements for a 500 kg horse (if that is its desired weight). In this example, the horse would only be fed about 115% of its current energy requirements and weight gain would be expected to be quite slow.

Feed Selection for Weight Gain

If we take a look at some feeds available to help put these calories into the horse, we'll recall that different feeds have different amounts of digestible energy per unit weight. For example, most types of hay will have approximately 1.7–2.2 Mcal per kilogram; cereal grains or commercially available concentrates will have a bit more than 3.2 Mcal/kg (depending on the type); and vegetable oil has about 9 Mcal/kg. What you feed can affect how quickly weight can be put on, but there are a few things to consider. For example, most horses won't consume buckets and buckets of vegetable oil, not to mention the "shiny" stools that may appear if a horse consumes more than two cups per day (shiny stools aren't necessarily a bad thing, but they do indicate that the oil isn't being absorbed effectively). Also, if we think about overall feed consumption, the upper limit for many horses is around 3% of their body weight;

they just won't eat more than that! Another thing to keep in mind is the fact that feeding high amounts of concentrates (especially those high in starch and sugar) is associated with digestive problems such as colic or metabolic issues such as laminitis and insulin resistance. So, while concentrates may have more calories per unit weight than hay, they might not be the best choice to include in the diet at high enough levels to induce weight gain.

The first step to having a horse gain weight is to increase its access to forage. This provides several benefits in that it is good and natural for the horse's digestive tract and can provide significantly more calories. If the horse has eaten all the hay by the next feeding, consider offering one more flake (approximately 1.5 to 2 kg, depending on the hay) at each feeding. If possible, offering "free choice" hay is the best option. This allows the horse to satisfy its foraging behavior and allows it constantly to have something in the stomach and digestive tract. Some horses, however, won't eat more hay if offered. In this case, an option is to offer something along the lines of hay cubes or roughage chunks. These products are essentially just hay, but in a different format, and they often "trick" horses into thinking they are getting some kind of concentrate. I've seen horses turn away any more hay but devour hay cubes. Just keep in mind that if you have an older horse, the hay cubes or roughage chunks may need to be soaked so the teeth can handle them (though an old guy would probably need his hay soaked as well). While hay cubes or roughage chunks are more dense and compact than hay, they are essentially similar from a nutrient content per unit weight (i.e., if you feed timothy cubes, they should be

Hay cubes can be tempting.

similar nutritionally to timothy hay based on weight).

If additional forage (any form) doesn't help put the pounds on, another option is to consider other fiber sources. Beet pulp (with no molasses to avoid sugar rushes) or rice bran is relatively high in calories (higher than forages) but is also high in fiber, so either is still a safe choice to include in your horse's diet. Wheat bran is another alternative, but it has such an inverted calcium-to-phosphorus ratio (about 1:9 rather than 2:1) that it can be tricky to feed (you need to ensure other sources of calcium get the ratio back up to 2:1).

Along with feeding various fiber sources, adding some oil to the diet is an easy and efficient way to add calories. Remember, fat has more than twice the (gross energy) calories as carbohydrates, so it is very energy dense. All oils are essentially equal in regard to their energy content; therefore if you are not looking for immune or inflammatory benefits, but simply to add some weight to your horse, the most inexpensive oil available at the grocery store will do. Recall that differences among oils depend on their chemical structure, the amount of double bonds between carbon units, and where these double bonds are placed. In addition to providing calories, the omega-3 fatty acids (such as found in fish or flaxseed oil) also have some immune function and hair coat benefits and likely some anti-inflammatory properties. One cup of oil (250 ml) has approximately 2.3 Mcal of energy and up to two cups can be easily fed to most horses. Some horses don't like oil, and some are finicky about the different types of oil (canola vs. corn vs. cocosoya oils). Introduce oil slowly by adding it to something such as beet pulp to encourage your horse to eat it.

Finally, if all else fails, offering true concentrates will provide more calories to the diet. Again, these preferably have more calories coming from fat and fiber than from starch and sugar. If you do choose to increase the amount of concentrates, it would be wise to consider introducing another meal feeding. For example, if you only feed twice a day, then each meal may be getting quite large (which may lead to digestive issues or wastage). Increasing the feedings to three

Practical Feeds to Add Calories

Feed:	Digestible Energy (DE)/kg	Amount to add 4 Mcal/day	Also Provides
Basic grass hay	~1.8 Mcal/kg	2.2 kg or ~1 flake	PVM
High-quality hay cubes	~2.2 Mcal/kg	1.8 kg	PVM
Vegetable oil	9 Mcal/kg	0.44 kg or ~1.7 cups	-
Beet pulp	2.9 Mcal/kg	1.38 kg	PVM
Sweet feed	~3.2 Mcal/kg	1.25 kg	PVM SS

*P = Protein; V = vitamins; M = minerals; SS = sugar and starch (careful!)

or four (or more) feedings per day will allow the individual meal sizes to remain the same.

If you have a horse in work that is on the thin side, the calories burned during a workout will counteract (at least some of) the calories in the diet. The calories required for maintenance (i.e., if you weren't trying to get your horse to gain weight) would be higher to account for the extra work effort (described in Chapter 7). Therefore, feeding upward of 25–35 Mcal/day might be required for a 500 kg horse to provide the calories for work *and* weight gain (depending, of course, on the level of work and the horse itself).

Some owners come across situations in which their horses simply won't eat enough or are picky about their feeds (assuming the lack of interest in various feeds isn't due to poor teeth quality or gastric ulcers, etc.). In these cases owners sometimes have to get creative. The science and nutrition behind feeding may have to go to the wayside and owners may need to offer any feeds a horse will eat.

For example, while sweet feed may cause problems with glucose and insulin dynamics, it is usually very palatable to all horses. Sweet feed and its associated sugar rushes, however, might make some horses "hot" and easily excitable, thereby actually expending energy and counteracting the extra calories in the diet. Some horses enjoy the taste of cocosoya oil or beet pulp, which are also options to increase caloric intake. Alfalfa hay may also be an option for some horses (if owners are careful about the excess protein) because it is extremely palatable. In many cases it is a bit of trial and error, though horse owners should remember to introduce new feeds slowly and not to expect results overnight. There are also some commercially available products marketed to improve weight gain. These are usually a mix of rice bran and vegetable oil and are often more expensive than buying the raw ingredients alone. They may be more palatable to some horses, though, and could be worth a try. Other high fat feeds that owners may find their horses enjoy include sunflower seeds and ground flaxseeds. However, there is little information regarding how much of these can be safely fed to horses.

Regardless of the type of feed chosen, the overall diet should still provide the required nutrients for your horse. Ideally, the only thing that should be fed above maintenance requirements is energy, though this is difficult to do when increasing overall feed intake. For example, if you tried to increase caloric intake through offering an additional 5 kg of hay, you would also be increasing the horse's protein intake and some vitamins and minerals (because these nutrients are also in hay). Horse owners should take a look at the whole diet to ensure all nutrients are being met and in appropriate amounts.

There are some concerns regarding calorie-to-nutrient ratios, such that increasing energy without increasing other nutrients may cause problems; however, this is more important with growing horses than mature horses.

CHAPTER 6

Feeding to Lose Weight or Body Condition

Because of the significant health risks associated with obesity in horses, owners may need to put their horses on a diet. This is a very difficult task to accomplish, in part not only because most horses are pets, and owners do not want to stress their pets, but also because feeding a balanced diet for all nutrients except for energy at rates sufficient to maintain a healthy digestive tract and satisfy feeding behavior is difficult. Feeding to obtain negative energy balance such that a horse will lose weight and body condition is not easy for either the owners or the horses, and takes time and commitment to the horse's overall well being.

Similarly to humans, the only way a horse can lose weight is to take in fewer calories than it expends. Therefore, it can consume fewer calories, expend more (through exercise), or combine the two methods.

Energetics of Weight Loss

We know from Chapter 5 on gaining weight that one body condition score requires a dietary energy intake difference of approximately 400 Mcal. As it does with gaining weight, feeding your horse to lose weight will take time. In fact, it will probably take more time for an animal to lose weight than to gain weight simply because we need to be more careful about drastically cutting calories for horses. So, rather than taking 100 days at reducing the intake by 4 Mcal per day, it may take 200 days with a reduction of 2 Mcal per day, or somewhere in between.

However, unlike offering more hay to help a horse gain weight, you can't just take hay away from a horse. Remember, horses need at least 1% of their body weight in forage, and feeding a lesser amount can cause some serious digestive problems. Furthermore, decreasing the amount of feed runs the risk of not providing enough "other" nutrients such as protein, vitamins, and minerals. For these reasons, simply reducing feed intake may not always be appropriate.

> ### AT A GLANCE
>
> ◆ Examine the entire diet to ensure all nutrient requirements (other than energy) are being met.
>
> ◆ Start reducing feed intake by reducing concentrate and pasture intake.
>
> ◆ Try to avoid reducing hay (or total feed) intake to less than 1.5% of body weight.
>
> ◆ Make all changes to a horse's diet slowly.

Also, there is often a question of whether a horse should be fed at his current requirements or at his desired weight. It is usually recommended that protein, vitamins, and minerals be fed at the current weight requirements while energy be fed at the desired weight requirements — and often at rates lower than that. Usually feeding between 70% to 90% of current energy requirements is enough to generate weight loss.

A recent study (van Weyenberg et al., 2008) examined feeding obese (BCS of 8–9) ponies to achieve weight loss. The desired rate of loss was approximately 1% of the ponies' goal weight per week (for example, if the goal weight was 200 kg, the ponies needed to lose 2 kg per week). The ponies were initially fed 70% of their energy requirements, but had to be further restricted to 35% to 50% of energy requirements to achieve the desired rate of weight loss. However, feeding below 70% of energy is not recommended unless under the strict supervision of a veterinarian. After losing an average of 16% of their initial body weight, the ponies had improved glucose metabolism and insulin sensitivity.

While not confirmed in the horse, it is well accepted in human nutrition that restricting energy causes the body to be more efficient in using it, thus making it even harder to lose weight. Therefore, it is possible that while it may take 400 Mcal difference to gain one body condition score, it may take a reduction of more than that to lose one body condition score. Exercise is also extremely important to increase the overall caloric expenditure by the horse, as discussed in Chapter 7.

Feed Selection for Weight Loss

When an owner wants a horse to lose weight, the first thing to do is look at its current diet very critically. Calculating the overall total intake may reveal that calories, and potentially even protein, vitamins, and minerals, are being fed above their requirements, similar to the example in Chapter 3. Often, the first thing that should be considered is removal (or decrease) of any grain or pasture access. Because grain mixes are usually fed to increase caloric intake, it seems logical that these mixes would not be required if a horse is being fed to lose weight. However, regular concentrate mixes may need to be replaced with some kind of "balancer" to replace any protein, vitamins, and minerals, especially if the hay is lower quality. (If the hay is decent quality, as determined by a hay analysis, you may be able to feed only a vitamin/mineral supplement). Recall that good-quality hay often provides enough calories and protein for most horses, but may have variable amounts of vitamins and minerals.

Pasture is often another "diet disaster," particularly if horses are allowed to graze freely. Horses are not very good at regulating feed intake and will often overeat if given the opportunity. Further, if you are counting your horse's calories, it is difficult to estimate feed intake from pasture, and therefore pasture caloric intake. A grossly obese horse should not have access to any pasture, while a moderately fat horse should have only limited access at most, either through management (reducing the hours per day a horse gets on pasture) or through the use of a grazing muzzle. Grazing muzzles effectively allow a horse the benefits of being at pasture (including the access for free exercise and social interaction with other horses)

A grazing muzzle can allow a modestly fat horse pasture time.

while limiting its ability to consume rich pasture grasses (including sugars and fructans). Many owners look at grazing muzzles as cruel contraptions, but for those who have seen a horse founder, grazing muzzles are a humane alternative.

With the prospect of removing or replacing grain in a diet, the hay needs to be examined carefully. A hay analysis will provide details about its nutritional quality, which is extremely important if you are going to be limiting intake. Often feeding hay at 2% of body weight will provide more calories than required, especially if the horse is not in work. Thus, it may be possible for some horse owners to reduce intake to 1.75% or even 1.5% of body weight. If total feed intake is reduced below 1.5% of body weight, it is possible that the horse may develop some boredom-related vices such as wood chewing or pawing. For horses with a history of such vices, it may be worth finding a hay source with lower nutritional quality (though still free of mold, dust, foreign objects, etc.). Lower nutritional quality hay could be fed in slightly higher amounts, potentially offsetting boredom. For example, moving from a hay with 2.2 Mcal/kg to 1.7 Mcal/kg means a horse needing 15 Mcal/day could get 8.8 kg of hay rather than 6.2 kg of feed (providing other nutrient requirements are met either with the hay or a balancer type of product). Some horses on limited feed intake may also exhibit coprophagia (the consumption of feces). While this is an abnormal behavior, it is not considered dangerous to the horse. Coprophagia does not necessarily mean the diet is lacking in nutrients (especially since the diet should have been carefully analyzed to ensure only energy intake is reduced) and is likely due to boredom.

Many horse owners have trouble with the idea of reducing a horse's feed intake, particularly if concentrate is removed. This is especially difficult if other horses in the facility are fed some kind of concentrate, and the overweight horse becomes stressed when not fed. However, owners can use a few tricks to appease their

Feeds such as beet pulp are useful for mixing with supplements.

dieting horses. Offering something like timothy hay cubes at feeding time can fool horses into thinking they are getting their meal without adding more calories to the diet (if you decrease hay fed to compensate for the cubes). Another method might be to offer some non-molasses beet pulp, especially if other supplements such as vitamin-mineral mixes need to be fed. In fact, it may be wise to feed an obese horse something such as a small amount of flaxseeds, due to the protein and omega-3 (anti-inflammatory properties that may be useful to counteract the obesity-associated inflammation) content. Also, many feed companies offer lower-calorie or even extruded types of feeds. Because of their low nutrient density (nutrients for a given volume), it is often possible to feed a small amount of these feeds without greatly offsetting the diet. Working with a nutritionist can help horse owners calculate the overall intake and determine what can be fed to optimize their horses' situation. Often, however, the horse owner just needs to be a little tougher.

As with all changes where diet and nutrition are integral, weight loss in horses should be gradual. Some potentially serious health consequences can result if horses lose weight too rapidly. Most notable is hyperlipemia, a condition characterized by excessive fat mobilization from the adipose tissue that results in high lipid concentrations in the blood (hyperlipidemia, with triglyceride concentrations being greater than 500 mg/dl) and can cause serious liver and kidney damage. Hyperlipemia is most common in animals such as donkeys and miniature horses, but can occur in all horses. Therefore, it is prudent to minimize stress during weight loss and to achieve the changes to the diet slowly. The rate of weight loss achieved in the pony study described earlier (van Weyenberg et al.) did not result in hyperlipemia and is therefore likely a safe rate of loss.

The best advice for horse owners to remember when looking to help their horses lose weight is to keep at it and to be tough. Though it may be difficult to have the fat pony muzzled and get limited feed, owners should realize it is in the horse's best interest.

Low-starch feed is recommended for insulin-resistant horses.

Feeding To Manage Insulin Resistance

It is possible that a horse may be insulin resistant but not outwardly obese, although in many cases the two occur concurrently. Insulin resistant (obese or lean) horses should be geared away from food with glucose as they can't use it effectively. Therefore, the diet should steer clear of high starch and sugar feeds, such as cereal grains and rich pastures. Getting hay, pasture, and grain analyses can indicate the sugar content of a feed, with the most common analytical tests being the NSC (non-structural carbohydrate) or NFC (non-fiber carbohydrate) fractions. It is recommended that horses diagnosed with insulin resistance be fed a diet with as low NSC as possible, ideally less than 10%. However, this is extremely difficult to achieve, as many grass hays have 8% to 12% NSC. Soaking hay (30–60 min) has been shown to reduce the sugars present by approximately 30%, and may be a required step for some owners. A hay analysis will let you know what kind of NSC values you have to work with, and it may be recommended that a different batch of hay be purchased. It has been shown that horses fed diets lower in starch and sugar (i.e., with more calories coming from fat and fiber) have higher insulin sensitivity than those consuming diets high in starch and sugar (Pratt et al., 2006). Exercise (if possible) is also very important for insulin resistant horses (See Chapter 7).

The Importance of Exercise

Over the ages horses have developed into excellent athletes. They have many unique adaptations that facilitate their ability to exercise. For instance, horses have a huge mass of skeletal muscle that is well adapted to long-distance exercise; they have a reserve blood supply to support oxygen carriage during exercise; and their ability to increase their heart rate and overall oxygen uptake almost eight-fold from rest is incredible compared to that in many other animals. This athleticism has made horses so useful to humans over the years, for work and for transport. Recently, however, the horse has been primarily used for sport and pleasure purposes. While obviously our elite equine athletes are a significant part of the horse industry, their contribution to overall horse population is small compared to those horses used for pleasure. There are a good number of horses competing on a national and local level that are primarily sport animals, but many of these horses are still "pets" to their owners and serve a dual purpose. The largest population of horses falls in the pet-pleasure category — horses ridden for pleasure, maybe with a few shows thrown in, but primarily companion animals. This population of animals appears to be most at risk for obesity. And as mentioned earlier (in Chapter 4), some disciplines reward horses with "extra condition."

Regardless of use or body condition, most horses could be exercised more. Assuming the animal is sound, it should be worked almost daily. This is especially important for overweight animals as exercise will increase the daily calorie expenditure more rapidly. Increased exercise combined with reduced calorie intake will hasten weight loss. Unfortunately, riding a horse at a decent level of work effort (either the length time of the ride, the frequency of the rides per week, or the intensity of a given ride) is time consuming and difficult for many horse owners to accomplish.

AT A GLANCE

◆ Exercise is the best way to hasten weight loss in horses.

◆ Exercise provides many health benefits to all horses.

◆ Introduce and increase exercise-training programs slowly.

◆ Cross-train your horse to reduce the risk of injury and to challenge him.

Health Benefits

Even for non-obese horses, exercise is extremely important for overall health. Not all horses, however, need to be ridden every day; some benefit from being lunged or worked in a round pen and others (especially older horses) do well with just free exercise in a large pasture (or dry lot). Nonetheless, exercise is extremely beneficial for a horse's overall health.

Exercise works many systems in the horse's body, most notably the cardiovascular, respiratory, skeletal, and muscular systems. Exercise causes an increase in heart rate, increased cardiac output (the amount of blood pumped per minute), and increased respiration, challenging the body systems to adapt and become more efficient. Skeletal bone is not a dead tissue; it is constantly being remodeled through the removing and depositing of calcium and phosphorus. Weight-bearing exercise stimulates remodeling and builds stronger bones. The muscle generates forces for movement and is highly adaptive to the stresses put to it. A horse trained for endurance types of exercise develops muscles more suitable for that type of work while a horse trained for high-intensity sprints endures muscular changes to fit those challenges. (It should be noted there are some genetic predispositions to the type of work a horse is most suited for; such as Quarter Horses being sprint animals and Arabians being endurance mounts.) In addition, exercise, particularly free exercise at pasture, is especially important for the overall mental well being of an animal.

Exercising obese horses has additional benefits. For instance, the calories burned during exercise can offset any required reductions in caloric intake and, therefore, you may not have to limit your horse's feed drastically. Alternatively, you can speed up the weight-loss effort through a combination of diet and exercise.

Exercise also has several metabolic benefits for obese horses. Because skeletal muscle is the largest user of glucose in the body, particularly through insulin stimulation, increasing the mass of skeletal muscle can greatly increase insulin sensitivity. Furthermore, exercise increases the number of glucose transporters (specifically the GLUT4 type that are insulin-sensitive to help move glucose across a cell membrane [Stewart-Hunt et al., 2006]). Thus, exercise not only increases the total quantity of insulin-sensitive tissue, namely skeletal muscle, but also increases the muscle's ability to use it. Several research studies have found a direct increase in insulin sensitivity through physical conditioning (Pratt et al., 2006; Stewart-Hunt et al., 2006). Exercise alone is often not enough, though; research in humans shows that adipocytokines (leptin and adiponectin) are only affected when exercise is accompanied by weight loss (due to adipose tissue loss).

In a practical example, Pagan and coworkers (2009), who examined body condition scores and insulin dynamics in sport horses, reported that pony hunters had significantly higher body condition scores than horses in other disciplines (such as show hunters or dressage horses). These ponies however had low incidence of hyperinsulinemia (only 8% of the ponies, compared to 50% of ponies with BCS greater than 7 reported by Carter et al., 2009), suggesting a protective effect of exercise, even in light of excess adipose tissue.

How Much Exercise

Exercise is particularly important for weight management. Often, owners want to see an increase in muscle development in addition to an overall decrease in fat coverage. There are many myths about feeding extra protein or various supplements to "build muscle," but if it were that easy, every person would have a lean stomach with "abs of steel." To build muscle, a horse (or person) must exercise and stress the muscles such that they adapt and get bigger to accommodate the stress. One of the key principles of exercise training is "overload" in that muscle must be pushed beyond its normal limits to effect changes. This overload can come from increasing the frequency of the workouts, the duration of the workouts, or the intensity of the workouts. Mind you, there is often a fine line between not enough work and too much work. Your veterinarian can help you decide how much exercise is suitable for your horse.

A trick for increasing workload for your horse without overdoing things is to "cross-train." Maybe do some hill work one day, some "sprints" another (10-second intervals at higher intensities, even at a trot if your usual ride is only at the walk), or even just a long hack through the woods. If you find you don't have the time for a full ride, try lunging your horse two times per day, rather than once. Remember, as with feeding, all changes, including an increase in exercise training, should be introduced slowly. If an owner doesn't have time to ride, a part boarder or trainer should be sought to help exercise the horse.

When working exercise into the overall equation of "calories in" vs. "calories out," we need to estimate how many calories are being burned. In general, higher intensities of work (trotting, cantering, hill work) will burn more calories per minute, but these intensities may not be maintained for long periods of time. One way to estimate the intensity of a workout is to monitor the heart rate. Equine heart rate monitors are readily available and can be worn while riding; some models can store information and track progress. As work intensifies, heart rate will increase. It should be noted however, that as a horse becomes fitter, his heart becomes more efficient and may be lower at a given work intensity after training compared to before training. Research has found that when the heart rate is 60 beats per minute (as it is at a walk), 24 kcal are burned per minute. Therefore, walking your horse for 30 min will burn 0.7 Mcal. A heart rate of 90 beats per minute (approximately a light trot) will burn 56 kcal per minute; 120 beats per minute (fast trot or slow canter) will burn 99 kcal/minute; 150 beats per minute will burn 158 kcal/min; and 180 beats per minute will burn 230 kcal/min (NRC *Nutrient Requirements of Horses*, 2007). Using a heart rate monitor and adding up the calories can help you estimate your horse's caloric requirements more accurately and adjust the caloric intake as required (for weight gain, maintenance, or loss).

A common problem for the owners of obese horses is that many of these horses are also lazy. This makes it particularly difficult to give them a hard workout. Many owners, therefore, look to nutritional changes or supplements to increase the "spirit" level of their horse (remember to avoid using the term energy, as energy refers to calories). Unfortunately, there are no products available to increase the motivation for a horse to be more active during a ride. Some

Varying the exercise routine can help increase workload.

owners look to feeding sweet feeds or other starch and sugar feeds in an effort to get the sugar rush associated with it. Remember that these sugar rushes are followed by a crash, and the potential risks associated with high starch and sugar intake (colic, metabolic issues) decrease the value of these feeds. And logically, offering an obese person a chocolate bar is not an encouragement to get off the couch and onto a treadmill. The best way to counteract a lazy horse is to get it fitter, through regular exercise (maybe with spurs or a crop). As horses lose weight, they will be able put more effort into the exercise and less into just carrying around their excess weight. Based on temperament and probably genetics, some horses are just lazier than others. This may make getting them to work difficult and also may make them prone to gain weight. Careful management and exercise training regimes will help these horses be the best athletes they can be.

Obviously there are going to be some horses that cannot exercise due to chronic lameness such as founder. However, these horses should still be able to walk (if not, euthanasia might be the only humane option). If they can walk, even hand walking (or walking with a rider on board) can help improve overall metabolism. These horses should also be housed in dry lots so they can get some free exercise (walking around the lot) but no additional feed from pasture.

Truths and Fallacies About Weight Management

In general, weight gain or loss is a matter of energetics and the first law of thermodynamics: Energy can neither be created nor destroyed, just converted from one form to another. Thus, energy within adipose tissue cannot be destroyed but must be converted to another form, such as energy used to contract the muscle during exercise. Therefore, within reason, weight gain or loss is simply a matter of caloric calculations. Every horse (or human) is different, and individual metabolism may not be accurately estimated, thereby confounding our calculations. Despite this fact, several companies claim to have products that magically add weight or reduce body fat.

Weight-Gain Products

There are numerous products out there to help horses gain weight. A careful examination of the contents likely reveals that one of the top ingredients is going to be some kind of high-fat ingredient (such as vegetable oil). If the overall calories in these products are estimated, it is probable they will be higher than the amount of calories in regular grain mixes, but less than those found in straight vegetable oil. Therefore, it may be cheaper and easier to feed your horse vegetable oil. However, if your horse is finicky and doesn't like straight vegetable oil, these products may be very worthwhile. In addition, many of these products use fat sources such as flaxseeds, so you may see a shinier coat as well. Thus, weight gain products can work to help your horse gain weight, but you may prefer just to add vegetable oil to your horses diet.

Many horse owners believe that if a horse is to gain weight, particularly muscle, they should increase the protein in the diet. Recall, however, that protein is not a very efficient energy source, and energy is what is required to create and store fat. Also, protein alone will not build muscle; work is required to do that. When a horse is put into work, its protein requirements will increase to help support muscle development, but this is usually easily met through increased feed intake to support the exercise itself. Therefore, just adding protein to a horse's diet will not help him gain weight.

> **AT A GLANCE**
>
> ◆ Try old-fashioned, time-tested methods of weight gain or loss — adjusting calories and altering exercise — first.
>
> ◆ Buyer beware: Many products out there have not been proven to work, but do solidly pad the wallet of the manufacturer. Do your research.

Weight-Loss Products

There are no simple solutions to losing weight (if there were, we wouldn't see such an obesity problem in our human population either); however, many products are marketed to help a horse lose weight and/or improve insulin sensitivity. One product commonly given to horses is thyroid hormone medication. The thyroid is a gland that produces hormones (thyroid hormones) that help regulate overall metabolism. If the thyroid gland is underactive (hypothyroid), it will not produce as many thyroid hormones in the system, thereby slowing the body's overall metabolic rate and predisposing an individual to gain weight.

It was once believed that all overweight horses were hypothyroid. However, this was usually untrue as the tests to measure thyroid hormone status in horses at the time simply weren't very accurate. These horses were often prescribed thyroid hormone medication to increase their metabolic rate and assist with weight loss. Thyroid hormone treatment can in fact help horses lose weight. One study examined the use of thyroid hormone medication in healthy normo-thyroid horses (horses with normal amounts of thyroid hormone being produced naturally) and found that these horses lost weight and had significantly increased insulin sensitivity following treatment (Frank et al., 2008b). Thus, there may be some benefit to such use of thyroid medications for extremely obese horses. It should be noted, however, that in humans, thyroid medication (especially when given to those who are not hypothyroid) is associated with cardiovascular complications and, therefore, not prescribed except in cases of hypothyroidism. The aforementioned equine study did not detect any cardiovascular issues (Frank et al, 2008a), but cardiovascular problems may still be a concern. With an extremely obese horse, the risk of laminitis may be greater than the risk of heart problems, and thyroid hormone medication may be useful. For most horses however, strict diet and exercise should be attempted first.

Several other human drugs are used to treat insulin resistance. Two studies have examined the effectiveness of one such drug, Metformin, on insulin sensitivity in horses, with conflicting results (Durham et al., 2008, Vick et al., 2006). Metformin appears to have low bioavailability in horses, compared to humans, which may explain why it hasn't proven to be effective in horses (Hustace et al., 2009). Additional work is required to examine the effectiveness of other potential drugs on horses.

Many other non-drug supplements are available to horses and believed to affect insulin sensitivity. However, because these products are not considered drugs, they are poorly regulated. There are a few key ingredients that may have some benefit to insulin sensitivity, although evidence in horses is lacking. Magnesium and chromium, as well as general antioxidants (such as vitamin C and E), are believed to have some function counteracting insulin resistance and possibly affect body weight. However, adequate clinical evidence is lacking in humans and no research in horses has reported any benefits (Guerrero-Romero and Rodriguez-Moran, 2005). Nonetheless, these nutrients (namely chromium and magnesium) likely won't

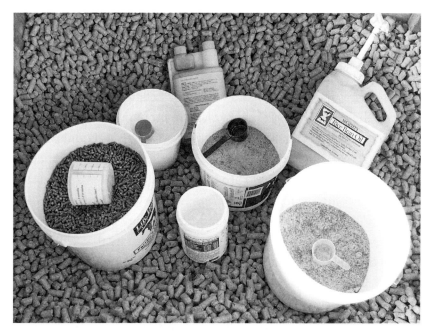

Many products claim to help horses lose or gain weight.

hurt the horse when fed in amounts according to instructions, so if economically feasible there is no reason not to try them. That said, they should not serve as a replacement for exercise and caloric intake restriction. Cinnamon and other herbal compounds are often fed to horses in hopes of improving insulin sensitivity. However, as reviewed by Tinworth et al. (2009), many herbal products do not have scientific research to support their claims, and many have not even been studied for safety in horses.

Many horse owners believe that weight can be gained or lost in specific physical locations, depending on diet. For example, some owners would prefer that fat be deposited along the buttock region to make the hindquarters appear larger and more developed, with fat being reduced along the crest of the neck. Similarly, some owners aim to "work" certain regions of the horse's body in attempt to reduce fat in that area. Unfortunately, there is no way to "spot reduce" in horses or humans; fat is lost approximately in equal amounts from all parts of the body, regardless of the exercise. However, genetics does play a role in determining what areas are more prone to store fat. This is highlighted in people where some carry their weight around the midsection and some carry excess weight in the hips and thighs (the apple vs. pear shape). It is possible that horses also have genetic predispositions to be either "crestier" — and carry fat around the crest of their neck — or to be more prone to developing a ridge down their back with excess fat coverage. It is unknown if there are greater health concerns associated with where a particular horse carries his fat, as there are in humans.

Another common misbelief among horse owners is that the hay belly results from a horse being too fat. The hay belly, or enlarged gut region in some horses, is mainly due to the fact that within this region lies the fermentative area of the large intestines. If a horse is offered relatively low nutritional quality feed, it is believed that the

Lower-quality hay can give a horse a hay belly.

intestines will retain the feed longer in effort to ferment it to a greater extent and to extract all possible nutrients. Thus, if the fermentative vat is more active, it stands to reason that the gut area would increase. One way to help counteract a hay belly is to decrease the required fermentation time by improving the quality of the forages. This may not be recommended, however, for overweight horses. It should also be noted that some horses simply have a larger gut region, and altering the diet won't affect it.

To avoid being misguided about weight gain or loss, horse owners are encouraged to educate themselves and research various compounds and products. Before purchasing a product, ask companies for publications of their study results proving the product's effectiveness. The Web site PubMed, provided by the National Institute of Health, is the database for human and veterinary scientific literature, and it is available to the public (www.pubmed.com). Owners can perform searches (on topics such as horse, insulin, obesity) to find out the latest research and information about treatments. Popular press publications such as *The Horse* often summarize research results in their health sections. While sources such as discussion boards and even advice from friends can be helpful, remember that even if something worked for one horse, it may not work for all. Veterinarians and nutritionists (ideally with a Master of Science or a Doctor of Philosophy graduate degree) are your best sources of information.

Frequently Asked Questions

Question: How do I know if my horse is the right weight?

Answer: There is no ideal weight for a horse of a given height, as things like breed and build can greatly affect weight. However, for a given height there is a likely a range of weights that correspond to good condition (fat coverage).

Q: What can I feed to make my horse gain weight?

A: There are many feed selections that contain calories that can contribute to weight gain in horses. The first thing to try is to simply offer more hay or other forage. If your horse is already eating free choice hay, then other high-fiber feeds such as beet pulp or even hay cubes, along with some vegetable oil, can pack on the pounds. Commercial "weight gain" products may be useful but are often more expensive than raw ingredients such as beet pulp or oil. Avoid feeding too much grain or concentrate, as these are associated with problems such as colic or laminitis.

Q: How do I get my horse to lose weight?

A: With patience! Losing weight, for horses and humans, takes time and commitment. Decreasing energy intake, through the restriction of things like pasture and grain mixes, to 70 percent of maintenance energy requirements is effective at reducing body weight and improving glucose metabolism. Exercise also helps to burn calories, hastening the weight loss efforts.

Q: My horse is lazy. Is there anything I can feed to give him more pep for our workout?

A: Unfortunately there isn't much in the way of feed that can cure a lazy horse — just as there isn't anything people can eat to make them less lazy for their workouts. High-sugar feeds (such as sweet feed, corn, or oats) may offer some short-term pep, but not without risk. The sugar rush associated with these feeds is short lived and is followed by a crash, and may predispose a horse to the development of insulin resistance. The best thing to do to "cure" a lazy horse is to get him into better shape so he'll be more suited to the level of work expected. A good set of spurs helps too.

Q: Does my horse need grain?

A: It depends. Grain is typically fed to increase the energy (calorie) content of the diet. Horses that are not in work or are overweight likely do not require additional energy, and most horses can derive most to all of their energy requirements from forage. Horses fed only forage may, however, require some kind of feed (balancer or vitamin-mineral supplement) to help supplement their protein, vitamin, and/or mineral requirements, depending on the quality of their forage.

Q: Is it cruel to put a muzzle on my horse or to put him in the "fat pen?"

A: No! In fact, anyone who has ever seen a horse suffer from laminitis knows that wearing a grazing muzzle or being in a dry lot is a much better alternative.

Q: How can I find out exactly how much energy and other nutrients my horse needs? How can I make sure his diet is perfectly balanced?

A: Working with an equine nutritionist (one who has graduate level training in equine nutrition) is the best way to get unbiased nutrition advice. When provided information about your horse (age, body weight, body condition score, overall health, activity level) as well as your feed (ideally with hay or pasture analysis and weights of any current feeds), a nutritionist can generally work through what your horse needs and how your feeds meet those requirements. They can suggest feeds that would meet any deficiencies and work with you to design a special weight-gain or weigh-loss program for your horse. If you prefer to do things on your own, working in a spreadsheet such as Excel can help you calculate all of the energy, protein, vitamins, and minerals that are currently in your horse's diet. Several books (the NRC's *Nutrient Requirements of Horses*, for example) can give you estimates of your horse's nutrient requirements.

Q: What is insulin resistance?

A: Insulin resistance is a condition in which the hormone insulin isn't effective at regulating blood glucose concentrations. This results in uncontrolled glucose concentrations and often very high amounts of insulin, both situations possibly contributing to laminitis. Insulin resistance may develop when horses consume diets high in starch and sugar, and/or with obese horses.

Glossary

Adipocyte — Fat cell

Adipose tissue — Fat tissue

Adiposity — Fat coverage

Amino acid — A small molecule containing nitrogen, carbon, hydrogen, and oxygen. There are approximately 20 different amino acids that differ based on their side chain. Amino acids are the building blocks of protein.

ATP — Adenosine triphosphate. The molecular unit of energy within cells of the body.

Balancer — A feed type that is fed in small amounts (ounces or grams) and provides vitamins and minerals and occasionally protein. These are fed to "balance" out hay that may have variable amounts of these nutrients.

Body condition score — A subjective score, often on a scale of 1 to 9, regarding the fat coverage on a horse. A horse with a score of 1 is emaciated and a horse with a score of 9 is grossly obese.

Calorie — A unit measurement of energy. A calorie (lower case "c") is the heat energy required to heat 1 gram of water by 1 degree centigrade. A Calorie (upper case "C") is 1,000 calories and is equivalent to a kilocalorie. Equine energy requirements and feed descriptions often utilize megacalories — or Mcal.

Carbohydrate (abbreviation CHO) — A class of molecules that includes sugars, starches, and fibers

Concentrate feed — A type of horse feed that has concentrated nutrients, such as energy or protein.

Coprophagy — The consumption of feces

Cytokine — Inflammatory protein

Diabetes — A condition in which the body either can't produce insulin or doesn't produce enough of it. Type 1 diabetes, the complete inability of the pancreas to produce insulin, occurs mostly in humans (though it has been reported in horses). Type II diabetes, often called adult onset diabetes in humans, is a reduced amount or lack of insulin production by the pancreas. This is most often a result of poor diet and/or obesity.

Digestible energy — The amount of energy that is actually available to the horse after accounting for fecal losses.

Energy — There are several interpretations. Food energy refers to the amount of calories a particular feed can generate, while energy requirements refer to how many calories an individual should consume. Mechanical energy is what the muscle uses to perform work.

Energy requirements — The energy requirements of a horse are based on its basal metabolic rate plus any additional energy required for work, growth, lactation, etc. Often referred to as digestible energy requirements.

Forage — Hay (and derivatives) and pasture consumed by horses

Grain — A crop seed that may be fed on its own (oats, corn, wheat, for example) or may be mixed with other feed ingredients to produce a horse feed.

Grass — A type of plant often used for pasture or hay. Examples include timothy, orchard grass, bluegrass, Bermuda grass, and fescue.

Hay — Grass or legume plant that is cut and dried to be fed to horses or other livestock.

Insulin — A hormone that regulates blood glucose concentrations. When blood glucose concentrations rise, such as after a meal, insulin is released from the pancreas. Insulin functions to facilitate the movement of glucose from the blood into tissues, thereby reducing blood glucose concentrations to baseline levels.

Insulin resistance — A condition in which insulin does not function properly in regulating blood glucose. This results in uncontrolled glucose concentrations in the bloodstream, which may contribute to laminitis.

Insulin sensitivity — Insulin's ability to function properly in regulating blood glucose concentrations.

Legume — A type of plant often used for pasture or hay. Examples include alfalfa, clover, and bird's foot trefoil. Legume hay (and pasture) tends to be higher in protein, calcium, and calories than those derived from grasses.

Lipid (fat) — A molecule that includes triglycerides and fatty acids, the components of cell membranes. With metabolism, fats can generate substantial amounts of energy (calories) per unit weight.

Protein — A class of molecules made up of amino acids that have functions in the body. Enzymes, hormones, structural proteins, etc.

Further Reading

Lewis, L.D., 1996. *Horse Feeding and Care*. Williams and Wilkins, Baltimore, MD.

National Research Council, 2007. *Nutrient Requirements of Horses*. National Academy Press, Washington DC.

References

Asplin, K. E., M. N. Sillence, C. C. Pollitt, and C. M. McGowan. 2007. Induction of laminitis by prolonged hyperinsulinemia in clinically normal ponies. *Vet. J.* 174: 530–535.

Carter, R., R. J. Geor, W. B. Staniar, T. A. Cubitt, and P. A. Harris. 2009a. Apparent adiposity assessed by standardised scoring systems and morphometric measurements in horses and ponies. *Vet. J.* 179: 204–210.

Carter, R., K. Treiber, R. J. Geor, L. Douglass, and P. A. Harris. 2009b. Prediction of incipient pasture-associated laminitis from hyperinsulinemia, hyperleptinemia and generalised and localised obesity in a cohort of ponies. *Equine Vet. J.* 41: 171–178.

Durham, A. E., D. I. Rendle, and J. E. Newton. 2008. The effect of metformin on measurements of insulin sensitivity and beta cell response in 18 horses and ponies with insulin resistance. *Equine Vet. J.* 40: 493–500.

Frank, N., B. R. Buchanan, and S. B. Elliott. 2008a. Effects of long-term oral administration of levothyroxine sodium on serum thyroid hormone concentrations, clinicopathologic variables, and echocardiographic measurements in healthy adult horses. *Am. J. Vet.* Res. 69: 68–75.

Frank, N., S. B. Elliott, and R. C. Boston. 2008b. Effects of long-term oral administration of levothyroxine sodium on glucose dynamics in healthy adult horses. *Am. J. Vet.* Res. 69: 76–81.

Garlinghouse, S. E., and M. J. Burrill. 1999. Relationship of body condition score to completion rate during 160 km endurance races. *Equine Vet. J.* Suppl. 30: 591–595.

Gentry, L. R. et al. 2002. The relationship between body condition, leptin, and reproductive and hormonal characterisitcs of mares during the seasonal anovulatory period. *J. An. Sci.* 80: 2695–2703.

Guerrero-Romero, F., Rodriguez-Moran, M. 2005. Complementary therapies for diabetes: The case for chromium, magnesium, and antioxidants. *Arch. Med. Res.* 36: 250-257.

Henneke, D. R., G. D. Potter, and J. L. Kreider. 1984. Body condition during pregnancy and lactation and reproductive efficiency of mares. *Theriogenology* 21: 897–909.

Henneke, D. R., G. D. Potter, J. L. Kreider, and B. F. Yeates. 1983.

Relationship between condition score, physical measurements and body fat percentage in mares. *Equine Vet. J.* 15: 371–372.

Hoffman, R. M., R. C. Boston, D. Stefanovski, D. S. Kronfeld, and P. A. Harris. 2003. Obesity and diet affect glucose dynamics and insulin sensitivity in thoroughbred geldings. *J. An. Sci.* 81: 2333–2342.

Hustace, J. L., A. M. Firshman, and J. E. Mata. 2009. Pharmacokinetics and bioavailability of metformin in horses. *Am. J. Vet. Res.* 70: 665–668.

Kane, R. A., M. Fisher, D. Parrett, and L. M. Lawrence. 1987. Estimating fatness in horses. In: Proceedings of the 10th Equine Nutrition and Physiology Symposium, Fort Collins, CO. p 127–131.

Kealy, R. D. et al. 2002. Effects of diet restriction on life span and age-related changes in dogs. *J. Am. Vet. Med. Assoc.* 220: 1315–1320.

Kearns, C. F., K. H. McKeever, K. Kumagai, and T. Abe. 2002. Fat-free mass is related to one mile race performance in elite standardbred horses. *Vet. J.* 163: 260–266.

National Research Council. 2007. *Nutrient Requirements of Horses.* National Academy Press, Washington, D.C.

Owens K, Pratt SE, Dowler L, and Cloninger, M. 2008. Basal insulin and glucose concentrations in horses of North Carolina. *J. An. Sci.* 86, E Suppl. 2: 431

Pagan, J. D., O. A. Martin, and N. L. Crowley. 2009. Relationship between body condition and metabolic parameters in sport horses, pony hunters and polo ponies. *J. Equine Vet. Sci.* 29: 418–420.

Phillips, L. K., and J. B. Prins. 2008. The link between abdominal obesity and the metabolic syndrome. *Curr. Hypertens.* Rep 10: 156–164.

Pratt, S. E., R. J. Geor, and L. J. McCutcheon. 2005. Repeatability of two methods for assessment of insulin sensitivity and glucose dynamics in horses. *J. Vet. Intern. Med.* 19: 883–888.

Pratt, S. E., R. J. Geor, and L. J. McCutcheon. 2006. Effects of dietary energy source and physical conditioning on insulin sensitivity and glucose tolerance in standardbred horses. *Equine Vet. J.* Suppl. 36: 579–584.

Pratt, S. E., P. D. Siciliano, and L. Walston. 2009. Variation of insulin sensitivity estimates in horses. *J. Equine Vet. Sci.* 29: 507–512.

Stewart-Hunt, L., R. J. Geor, and L. J. McCutcheon. 2006. Effect of short-term training on insulin sensitivity and skeletal muscle glucose metabolism in standardbred horses *Equine Vet. J.* Suppl. 36: 226–232.

Thatcher, C. D. et al. 2007. Prevalence of obesity in mature horses: An equine body condition study. In: The American Academy of Veterinary Nutrition 7th Annual Clinical Nutrition and Research Symposium, Seattle, Washington. p 6.

Tinworth, K.D., Harris, P.A., Sillence, M.N., and Noble, G.K. 2009. Potential treatments for insulin resistance in the horse: A comparative multi-species review. *The Vet. J.* DOI: 10.1016/tvjl.2009.08.032.

Treiber, K., D. S. Kronfeld, and R. J. Geor. 2006. Insulin resistance in equids: Possible role in laminitis. *J. Nutr.* 136 (7 Suppl): 2094S–2098S.

Van Weyenberg, S., M. Hesta, J. Buyse, and G. Janssens. 2008. The effect of weight loss by energy restriction on metabolic profile and glucose tolerance in ponies. J. *An. Physiol. An. Nutr.* 92: 538–545.

Vick, M. M. et al. 2007. Relationships among inflammatory cytokines, obesity and insulin sensitivity in the horse. *J. An. Sci.* 85: 1144–1155.

Vick, M. M. et al. 2006. Obesity is associated with altered metabolic and reproductive activity in the mare: Effects of metformin on insulin sensitivity and reproductive cyclicity. *Reprod., Fert., and Dev.* 18: 609–617.

Wyse, C. A., K. A. McNie, V. J. Tannhil, J. K. Murray, and S. Love. 2008. Prevalence of obesity in riding horses in scotland. *Vet. Rec.* 162: 590–591.

Index

A

adenosine triphosphate (ATP)... 23–26
adipose tissue 57, 58, 59, 64, 66,
　　　　　　　　　81, 86, 90
adiposity, measures of
　body mass index (BMI)...............17
　girth-to-height ratio (G:H)...........17
　ultrasound..................................17
alfalfa 29, 36, 40, 45, 46, 49, 69
amino acids 25–26, 36, 43

B

balancer......................45, 78, 80, 97
Barbaro...59
basal metabolic rate........................30
beet pulp........ 30, 41, 44, 48, 61, 73,
　　　　　　　　75, 80, 81, 96
Bermuda grass................................40
blood glucose 48, 59–64
body condition 8, 10–15, 18–21,
　　　　　　　　54–58, 64–65, 69–70
body mass index (BMI) 17
body measurement 8–10
body weight 8–10, 18–19, 20, 31, 32,
　　　　　　　　35, 44–46, 62, 70–71,
　　　　　　　　77–79, 92, 96
　equations for..................................9
broodmares......19, 44, 45–46, 55, 65

C

calcium.... 37, 40, 41, 42, 45, 51, 53,
　　　　　　　　73, 85
calories 22–24, 41, 47–48, 70–71,
　　　　　　　　73–74, 78, 87–88
carbohydrates ... 23–24, 26, 36, 53, 73
　disaccharide................................24
　monosaccharide...........................24
　polysaccharide.............................24
cereal grain......24, 41–42, 47, 61, 71

cinnamon.......................................93
colic 66, 72, 89, 96
commercially available feeds 37, 41,
　　　　　　　　42–43, 46, 75
concentrates.....46–49, 58, 69, 71–73
copper..................................... 37, 53
coprophagia...................................80
cresty neck scores (CNS)...............16
　See also body condition

D

diabetes ....59, 60, 63–64, 99, 101.
　See also insulin resistance
dietary intake...........................50–52
digestible energy 26–30, 70
digestive system 27–30, 44, 49
　cecum 27
　colon...28
　large intestine 27–29, 94
　small intestine......................27–29
dry matter 29, 53

E

"easy keeper" 30, 32, 61
emaciation 54–56
　causes of................................55–56
energy 22–33, 97
　digestible 26–30
　energetic compounds........... 23, 26
　gross 26
　weight gain............................69–71
　weight loss............................76–78
energy feeds 29–30, 41
energy requirements.................30–33
Equine Metabolic Syndrome..........59
euglycemic-hyperinsulinemic clamp ... 63
exercise...................... 58, 78, 84–89
　benefits of..................................85

F

fats............................... 23, 25, 36
  omega fatty acids.................. 25, 36
  triglycerides............................ 25
feeds 39–44
  commercially available 42–43
  energy feeds 41
  forage.....................................39–40
  quality...49
  weight of.....................................50
fiber 25, 29, 36, 44, 48–49, 52, 73
flaxseed 36, 43, 81, 90
foals.................................9, 10, 43, 55
forages.....30, 39–40, 44, 46, 69, 72–73
founder 59, 62, 79, 89

G

genetics 61–62, 85, 93–94
girth-to-height ratio (G:H) 17, 18
glucose 47–48
  See also blood glucose
glucose tolerance test 63
glycemic index (GI) 61
grains................................ 30, 49, 97
grazing muzzle 78–79, 97
growing horses 10, 32, 44, 45, 75

H

"hard keeper"...31, 32, 68, 71, 74–75
hay......39–40, 44–46, 49–50, 72–73,
                                    79–81
hay belly....................................94–95
hay cubes.......................... 39, 72, 81
haylage 39
hay sample 40–41, 79, 82
heart rate.................... 84, 85, 87, 88
heat tolerance 55, 66–67
Henneke Body Condition Scoring
  (BCS) 10–15, 57
  See also body condition
hyperglycemia..............................60

hyperinsulinemia.........60, 62, 63, 86
hyperlipemia 81
hypothyroid.............................91–92

I

ideal weight................ 18–21, 30, 96
insulin resistance 16, 48, 59–65, 72,
                        82–83, 92, 98
  consequences of 63–65
  diagnosis of 62–63
  feeding to manage 82
  genetics..................................61–62
insulin sensitivity 48, 86, 91–93
  See insulin resistance
intestinal malabsorption syndrome.... 55
intestines ... 27–29, 44, 48, 55, 60, 66, 94
iron 37, 53

L

lactating mares.... 31, 32, 34, 35, 44, 46
laminitis...................... 48, 59, 63–65
laziness....................... 88–89, 96–97
leptin 64, 65, 86
lipids. *See* fats
lipomas.................................. 55, 66
lysine...36

M

magnesium 37, 53, 92
maintenance level... 30, 31, 35, 45, 51,
                74, 75, 88, 96
Metformin 92
Microsoft Excel....................... 50, 98
minerals...........37, 42–43, 45, 47, 53
  macro 37, 53
  trace 37, 45, 53
molasses feeds 47, 60
muscle 18, 56, 85–87, 91

N

National Animal Health Monitoring
  System (NAHMS)..............57

National Research Council 30, 34
Nutrient Requirements of Horses ...30, 34, 38, 88, 98
nutrients................ 34–39, 50–52, 97
  fats and carbohydrates.................36
  minerals.......................................37
  protein 35–36
  vitamins..................................37–39
  water......................................34–35
nutritionist..... 33, 47, 50, 55, 58, 69, 81, 97

O

obesity 52, 57–59, 61–66, 76, 86
  causes of.................................57–58
  health issues 58–67
oil. *See* vegetable oil
older horses 20, 44, 56, 66, 85
omega-3 fatty acids 25, 36, 43, 73
omega-6 fatty acids 36
overweight..... 17, 18, 57, 80, 84, 91, 95, 97. *See also* obesity

P

pasture...35, 39–40, 44, 52, 58, 78–79
performing horses 20–21, 32, 84
phosphorus 37, 41, 42, 45, 51, 53, 73, 85
ponies 17, 18, 21, 30, 61, 63, 77, 86
potassium 37, 53
protein 29, 35–36, 43, 45–46, 91
proteins............................ 23, 25–26.
  See also amino acids
PubMed.......................................95

R

rice bran ... 41, 42, 44, 48, 61, 73, 75

S

salt block 35, 37, 45
scales...8
selenium 37, 47, 53

sodium.................................... 37, 53
stallions 31, 32, 62
starch................................. 48, 53, 61
subcutaneous fat..................... 17, 64
sugar rush 47–48, 75, 89, 97–98
sugar..........24, 28, 48–49, 53, 79, 82
supplements..............43, 46, 80, 81, 87, 88, 92
sweet feed..................42, 60, 75, 96

T

Tevis Cup 20
The Horse...................................95
thyroid.....................................91–92
timothy hay 44, 45, 46, 51, 73, 81

U

underweight.............................17, 54
  See also emaciation
U.S. Department of Agriculture.....57

V

vegetable oil .. 29, 41, 48, 71, 75, 90, 91, 96
visceral fat....................................64
Vitamin A.....................................39
Vitamin B complex 37
Vitamin C................................ 37, 92
Vitamin D....................................38
Vitamin E 36, 37, 39, 47, 92
Vitamin K....................................37
vitamins................ 37–39, 41–43, 47
  fat-soluble................................37
  water-soluble 37
volatile fatty acids (VFAs) 25, 28

W

water....................................34–35
weigh tapes.............................. 9, 10
weight gain........................ 68–75, 96
  feed selection........................71–75
  products................................90–91

weight-gain products......... 90–91, 96
weight loss 76–83, 96
   consequences of 81
   exercise.................................85–86
   feed selection.........................78–81
   products 91–95
weight-loss products 91–95

Y

yearling 45

Z

zinc... 37, 53

Photo Credits

CHAPTER 1

Anne M. Eberhardt, 19, 20.

CHAPTER 2

Anne M. Eberhardt, 30-32.

CHAPTER 3

The Horse magazine, 40; Lori Schmidt, 50.

CHAPTER 4

Shannon Pratt-Phillips, 56; courtesy of the author, 65
Anne M. Eberhardt, 66.

CHAPTER 5

The Horse magazine, 68, 72; Paula da Silva, 70.

CHAPTER 6

Anne M. Eberhardt, 79; The Horse magazine, 80, 82.

CHAPTER 7

Anne M. Eberhardt, 88.

CHAPTER 8

Anne M. Eberhardt, 93, 94.

PHOTO WELL

Anne M. Eberhardt, Cynthia LaRose; Pam McKenzie;
Paula da Silva, The Horse magazine.

ILLUSRATIONS
ROBIN PETERSON, DVM

COVER PHOTO
DUSTY PERRIN

About the Author

Shannon Pratt-Phillips grew up in Toronto, Ontario, where she spent her evenings and weekends riding hunters. After completing her bachelor of science in nutritional science from the University of Guelph, she attended the University of Kentucky to pursue her master of science in equine nutrition. After returning to Canada, she obtained her PhD from the University of Guelph in the field of equine nutritional physiology. She is currently an assistant professor at North Carolina State University in  the Department of Animal Science. Her teaching efforts are in equine science, equine nutrition, and physiology of domestic animals. Her research focuses on glucose metabolism, insulin sensitivity, and weight management in horses.